Minimalism

Ultimate Guide Towards Focused Life
And Live Better With Less Technology

*(Learn How To Simplify, Declutter, Reduce Stress,
Find Happiness)*

Clara Norman

Published By **Elena Holly**

Clara Norman

All Rights Reserved

Minimalism: Ultimate Guide Towards Focused Life And Live Better With Less Technology (Learn How To Simplify, Declutter, Reduce Stress, Find Happiness)

ISBN 978-1-77485-626-0

No part of this guidebook shall be reproduced in any form without permission in writing from the publisher except in the case of brief quotations embodied in critical articles or reviews.

Legal & Disclaimer

The information contained in this ebook is not designed to replace or take the place of any form of medicine or professional medical advice. The information in this ebook has been provided for educational & entertainment purposes only.

The information contained in this book has been compiled from sources deemed reliable, and it is accurate to the best of the Author's knowledge; however, the Author cannot guarantee its accuracy and validity and cannot be held liable for any errors or omissions. Changes are periodically made to this book. You must consult your doctor or get professional medical advice before using any of the suggested remedies, techniques, or information in this book.

Upon using the information contained in this book, you agree to hold harmless the Author from and against any damages, costs, and expenses, including any legal fees potentially resulting from the application of any of the information provided by this guide. This disclaimer applies to any damages or injury caused by the use and application, whether directly or indirectly, of any advice or information presented, whether for breach of contract, tort, negligence, personal injury, criminal intent, or under any other cause of action.

You agree to accept all risks of using the information presented inside this book. You need to consult a professional medical practitioner in order to ensure you are both able and healthy enough to participate in this program.

Table of Contents

Chapter 1: Minimalism's Benefits 1

Chapter 2: Living A Minimalist Lifestyle . 16

Chapter 3: Why It Is Important To Set Some Goals 27

Chapter 4: Minimalism And Clutter 41

Chapter 5: Arranging And De-Cluttering Laundry And Washroom 53

Chapter 6: Living A Minimalistic Life 61

Chapter 7: How Can You Be One? 74

Chapter 8: Why Do We Clutter Our Lives? 80

Chapter 9: Why Do We Clutter Our Lives? 89

Chapter 10: Minimalist Home Decorating 98

Chapter 11: Decluttering Mind 105

Chapter 12: Decluttering Guest Rooms & Bedrooms The Minimalist Method 115

Chapter 13: Think Small, Live Big 130

Chapter 14: Cultivating Digital Minimalism Behaviors 140

Chapter 15: How To Organize Your Home Office 153

Chapter 16: Minimalism And Fashion .. 164

Conclusion 176

Chapter 1: Minimalism's Benefits

Minimalist living can bring you many benefits, some of which may not be apparent when you first embark on your journey. Your minimalist lifestyle and the values that you have developed will carry over to other areas of your lives. The personal and mental benefits of becoming a minimalist will be evident in your daily life. You will have more space in the house, and you will feel less stressed.

A minimalist lifestyle can help to reduce your carbon emissions and improve the environmental quality of your surroundings. You may also find that your minimalist lifestyle can help others. It can teach you how minimalism can work, and even allow you to give your old items away to people in need.

You have more space

It can make your space appear smaller than it really is by cluttering and storing too much furniture. You can think back to when you first moved into a home. Remember the feeling of walking from one room in the other. Most likely your home felt spacious, open, and large.

Next, imagine how you organized your belongings in your new home. You may have noticed that you had too few kitchen items and too little storage space. I find that it is my problem every time I move into new places.

There are many things that people don't use in their homes, and it can make the space feel small or cramped. You can reduce clutter and create the space you have always wanted by living a minimalistic lifestyle.

You Stress Less

Anxiety and stress can result from clutter. If you have many possessions and are trying to organize them or try to find something, you will become more stressed and anxious. This happens when you need to move objects around your house. Cortisol manages your stress levels.

If you're constantly being bombarded with cortisol every time you need organize your home so that you can move about your home, your stress and anxiety levels will go up. If your cortisol levels continue to rise while you are constantly surrounded in clutter, this can have a negative impact on your health.

Paranoia, tension, and other factors can all contribute to stress and anxiety. People get anxious when they are unable to find something, and paranoia when they have high-value possessions. If you have too much clutter, you'll feel stressed when you don't get what you want. If you lack security in your home, or live with people who are less concerned about your possessions, you might become paranoid about their safety when you are not at home.

Decluttering can help you take inventory of all the things in your home. You can decide if these items are valuable and worth keeping or if you don't use them often enough to get rid of them. You can also identify important items and determine safe storage solutions. For example, you could clean out your clutter in a cupboard or drawer, place your essential items inside, and lock it once you're done. You can lower your cortisol levels and feel less anxious about leaving the house.

Cleansing your home is easy

The dust that builds up from clutter and furniture in your house will cause it to be harder to clean. Cleaning can be difficult when you live with your parents, siblings, or children. Decluttering and getting rid bulky furniture will make your space easier to maintain and will save you time. Minimal furniture is easier to clean.

You produce more and procrastinate fewer

You may associate each possession with a certain emotion, memory or feeling when you touch or look at it. One example is a souvenir you received from your partner while they were on vacation, or a magazine sitting on your desk. There are many things you can look at, and interact with, when you're surrounded by clutter. Each of these memories and emotions can take some time and energy.

If you have anything that distracts you, your productivity drops and you'll find yourself procrastinating instead of working on the task at hand. Similar to the above, if your home seems messy or cluttered you might feel the urge to clean it.

Clean, tidy, and simple surroundings can help you increase productivity and decrease procrastination. You can also reduce distractions by making sure that your house is clean before going to sleep. You will find that there is no other thing you can concentrate on while you work.

You have more time to do the things that matter

It can be hard to see the future when your past is reliving or distracting you. You may find yourself focusing on the things you've done in the past with people and how they treated you.

For example, you might get up with your partner, children, and prepare for the day. You go home, get the kids off to school, then you return home, prepare dinner, and then you go to sleep. You might have moments when you do briefly acknowledge your partner or children during the day. However, you might not take time to enjoy one another's company and spend some time together.

If you get rid of clutter and other items that may distract you or tie your heart to the past, you'll find you have more time to be with your family and enjoy the things that you love. You never know what you may discover, but you may discover a passion that you had while you were free, which you need to share with others.

You Have More Choice

It can be difficult to overcome debt and valuable possessions that leave us with little money each month. These possessions can tie us back to the past. They force us to continue living our lives each month in the same manner so we can pay off these debts. Our possessions can be thrown out and we can enjoy the things we enjoy.

If you are passionate about traveling and feel overwhelmed by your possessions then you should declutter your home and sell or give them to someone who is going to treasure them just like you. You'll be able to travel further and you won't worry about your possessions home.

Decluttering your space and selling any items you have will help you eliminate debts and allow you to live a happier and more fulfilling life. Decluttering your space and selling your items can allow you to pursue the job you love, but it will also help your financial situation.

You can be focused on what you love

While we all work hard each month to maintain our lifestyles, we rarely have enough money or time to spend on ourselves, our hobbies, or other extracurricular activities. Decluttering and selling off items can give you more money at the end the day so you can enjoy what you love doing and pay off your outstanding debts. Adopting simple living methods will allow you to reduce your monthly spending on goods.

Doing this will help you realize how much less you could make. This can let you focus on the things you truly love. There are many options to reduce your work hours. You could also look into working part time or taking a chance on a career that may pay less, but offer more reward. Follow your dreams and you will find peace in your heart and soul. You'll also be happier.

Donate to Others

It will be easy to see how many items you don't use anymore when you start decluttering your home. You might think about donating your unwanted possessions to other people. If you aren't interested in making money from your unwanted possessions, then you can feel good about yourself by donating them to others. These feelings can motivate you and encourage you to keep clearing out your home so that more people are able to smile when they use them.

Influence Others

Decluttering your space and living a simpler life are the best parts. When you invite friends over, they will see how beautifully your space looks. A beautiful home decorated with no clutter is appealing to be admired. You might find that you inspire them to live a simpler, more minimalist lifestyle after they return from abroad.

You Can Support Causes

By living a simpler life and saving money, you can support causes you feel strongly about. If the hospital is in need of blankets for children's hospitals, you could go to the store and purchase wool, and then spend your free time making blankets. Donate any items that are no longer needed, like toys for children. You can also donate food to those in need. If you do this, it will bring you joy knowing you are making a difference and helping those in need.

You'll Have More Money

A minimalist lifestyle and learning to buy with intent will help you be less likely buying things out of impulse. It is easy to be blindsided by the pressure of consumer buying, and the need for material possessions that society demands. Most of us buy things we see on TV and go to the shops in search of that item. Once you learn to be a minimalist and get a better grasp of what is in your home and how it comes out, you'll begin to question the reasons you bought something.

This will make you more financially responsible and help you buy smarter. You shouldn't give up on your desire to spoil yourself, but this will allow you to be more conscious about the things you purchase. You will find that you stop going to the shops as often and you will spend less time there.

Most of us have more clutter in our homes than what we need. You might find things you don't need, but that are still useful. You may also discover that you no more need the bookcase or dresser in an area of your home after decluttering. If this happens, you might be able to put the furniture or other items up for sale so that others will have access to them.

Save Money

Make a conscious choice to not spend money on unnecessary items or sell unwanted things after decluttering your home. You may be surprised at how much money you have left over at the end. This money can be put away for a rainy days or saved up for something you've had your eye for for a while. While it might seem overwhelming at first to adopt a minimalist lifestyle and not buy anything, each purchase that you make adds up.

Before you tried to live a minimalistic lifestyle, you might have had to spend a small amount to get furniture and other accessories. You may have ended up with furniture or other items that are less than satisfactory and could break easily. This will force you to buy another. You can save money on furniture and other things by putting aside the money that you earn each month.

It makes your life happier

Simple living and a clutter-free home will help you be happier and live a healthier life. You will feel accomplished when you have more money at your end of the month and save more for the things you really want. You won't feel like you are only working each month to pay back your debt and expenses. Minimalism helps you eliminate debt and allow you to live a simpler life.

If you become a minimalist, it will be easier to manage your stress at work. You'll also notice a boost in your mood, which can help you feel more relaxed and at ease about your job.

Your monthly savings can go towards helping others in need. You could also sell your furniture or items to people who treasure them, and give them to the less fortunate. You can feel great about yourself, make a difference, and even find a new purpose by supporting other causes.

It improves your health

Minimalism can improve your health. Minimalism can improve your health. This stress can be detrimental to your body. Long-term exposure to stressful environments can also lead to mental disorders such as depression, anxiety, or personality disorders.

Clutter and hoarding can make you sick

Stress and clutter can lead to illness. Dust, mold, and hairs can be hard to see if you have many possessions or a large property. It's possible to not see that mold has grown behind furniture or boxes.

These are dangerous things that can cause you to get very sick. It is dangerous to inhale the mold spores. Many people also have allergies to dust. This can lead long-term health problems like an increased risk of developing asthma and worsening allergy symptoms.

Also, clutter can cause mental havoc. It can lead to anxiety and frustration. There are those who live with so many possessions that it severely limits their mobility, weight, or cripples their physical health. Hoarders at this extreme must climb over and set their things aside to be mobile and complete basic household tasks.

People can become more mobile and gain weight. This can lead a person to have mental health problems that can cause them to become more isolated. Without professional help, it can be very difficult to get your life back on track.

Chapter 2: Living A Minimalist Lifestyle

There are many ways you can start minimalism. The most important thing is to decide whether you want it to be a serious endeavor or if you just want to have fun. I recommend planning for the changes you'll make in your life. There are many ways to minimize, but there is one goal that everyone is working towards. Because of this common ground, we have certain methods that help us stay on track.

Realistically, minimalism is not for everyone. Don't get discouraged if minimalism isn't something you can do easily. Pushing yourself too hard can make it impossible to go down this path. Do not force it if it is not natural. Instead, accept what you can handle and take small steps forward instead of taking big leaps. There is nothing wrong with pace and slow wins marathons.

These tips can help you get off to the right start and ensure that you don't fail. Use them as much or little as you wish and try your best to implement them all.

Tip #1 Practice makes perfect

To start, you must learn to let yourself go. As you get more experience, it will become second nature. It might be hard to learn, but it will get easier the more you practice.

The hardest part about this is remembering that you are a minimalist. It's important to declutter your space frequently, be mindful of what you take on and keep your life organized. Similar to how you practice your guitar every single day, you should also make an effort every day to practice minimalism. Otherwise, you will lose muscle memory.

Even if this happens, it is possible to become overwhelmed and realize that minimalism has not been a priority for you. A consistent effort to keep on top is the best way for minimalism to be maintained and started. You don't have to tidy up your house every day. One of your daily practices could be to clear out your emails and notify you, or to meditate to unclutter your mind.

Tip #2, Question Everything

You don't need to live in paranoia, or grab your tinfoil cap and go crazy. There should be a way for you to identify what matters in your life. This will make it easier to declutter and eliminate any doubts. This can be done by setting up a set or criteria to measure the value of what you own, how you interact with others, and how you feel about your energies.

If you are unsure which things to get rid of, the easiest question is, "does it bring you joy?" Is this empty joy? Are you feeling sentimental? Is the sight of it making you happy? You don't necessarily have to fix everything, but understanding why they are valuable will help give you a better sense of their worth.

If the answer is "No", you might have to think about whether it's important to you. Maybe you need it to go to school, or to work. Maybe it's a key that could be useful in the future. It should be kept if it serves some purpose. If not, get rid.

If the product doesn't meet your needs but you find it useful, another question to ask is: "Do you have enough of this?" This applies for everything, including clothing, cutlery/decor, office supplies etc., as well any medicine or tools. Don't give away the one screwdriver you only have. If you have three of the exact same items, but only one screwdriver, it's time get rid of them all.

This will allow you to make two key changes.

* You'll determine what doesn't make you happy.

* It's impossible to get used up for things that have no purpose.

Most people are materialistic only because they have been trained to. Maintaining a sharp eye and asking questions will give you a fresh outlook on what is going on in your life. To make space for what matters, you will have to decide if it's good or not for you.

Tip #3. Set goals and make sure to review them often

Although you will need to have a game plan, it is not essential. It's unlikely that a football team will use the same strategy to defeat every opponent. And you shouldn't stick with a plan you wrote when you were a different person. Blueprints are great, however they're only meant to be a base. Blueprints only serve a purpose if they are used as a foundation. How can you make your game plan easy to review?

You can do what you want, just like minimalism. The most important thing is that you have goals that are achievable and that you feel motivated to keep them. There are several ways you can make this easier.

First, you'll want to create an easy plan that you can reference later. It is great to keep an organized journal, explaining your goals in detailed detail, but it might be difficult to look through it when it comes to reminders of the important things.

Once you find a good medium or system to help you list your goals take some time to ponder the content. Consider what drove you to become a minimalist. Take the time to write down your motivations so that you can recall them if you ever feel like you are missing something.

Next, create a list or spread that lists the essentials for your life. This will be your inventory. It can be used to cross-reference things you don't want, those that make you unhappy, and, of course, the ones that should be there.

This master list will help you to track your progress and keep you on track.

Keep in mind that the document isn't fixed in stone. It can be changed to suit your needs and views. It is meant to keep the you grounded, and not to trap you.

Tip 4: Declutter Everything

This is the place where your muscle memory steps in. Minimalism can be thought of as getting rid or reducing the amount of stuff you don't use. But minimalism has deeper roots. You could think of it as redesigning the way you live. This is a time to reconsider everything you own and use as well as everyone you have contact with. Although it sounds harsh, it is a necessary step toward minimalism.

The golden rule is: Get rid of it if it's not useful and meaningless.

This is applicable to virtually everyone. These are just some examples of how this can be done.

Cleaning up Online Accounts

Curating the personalities you pay close attention to is a form or minimalism. It will be clear that quality is better then quantity.

Also, delete any emails that you no longer need. Get rid of unnecessary apps and documents. It's a great idea to optimize your notification settings so your phone/computer doesn't pester you with nonsense every ten secs. To ensure that you aren't feeling responsible for not checking your mailbox at another time, you can also set an alarm to notify your phone or computer when you need it.

It is a good idea to unsubscribe all vloggers which consume too much of your time. You shouldn't spend more that 30 minutes watching these videos.

Rethink your relationships

Interacting in person is an exchange for energy. If this happens, don't waste your time or energy on people who are not fulfilling you. Although it may sound harsh, it's actually not. It's an act in self-preservation. You don't have have to make them feel horrible or hurt their feelings. But you don't have a duty to keep them around. People are just like other things. They either have value for you or they don't.

After you have eliminated the unkind, irritable, and harmful people in your inner circle, you will have more energy for the people you love and desire. You'll have more energy to nurture the people you love and less to water the artificial relationships.

Organize Your Workspace

Make sure to get all your ducks together. You need to organize your files, drawers as well your briefcase, desk, phone, and office supplies. Our workspaces are most at risk of clutter. After all, we work hard, so it's natural that they can become cluttered. It's easy to make a beautiful, tranquil garden into a swamp when we neglect it.

Remember that evidence clutter can increase stress levels and cause it to worsen. Your workspace is the place where stress should not exist. However, it is also the place where we experience stress the most. The two are interconnected. Do you?

Take care of your home

Your home is likely to be in good shape. Our homes are our happy places. Although I can't promise that my home won't look like a tornado, it's possible I'll find you and have you stay with me while I clean it. I can't resist becoming a cleaning expert!

Do not be embarrassed to clean up your house. You can start by clearing out your entire house and then go through it with a fine-tooth comb. Here's what to concentrate on:

* Wardrobes: Clothes and Shoes

* Your basement

* Your attic

* Grocery shelves, fridges, freezers, pantries or pantry

* First Aid kits and Medicine cabinets

* Desks/tables, shelves and wall units

* Garages, workshop, and toolboxes

* Makeup, cosmetics and toiletries

* Kitchenware and furniture.

Simplify your Schedule

What you do matters just as much as what it is. Decluttering both your time and your space is key. Recognize why you are so busy, and what you can do to make your space more accessible for the things you value. If you're not required to attend (such as doctor's or work meetings), cancel. It's amazing how much you can save time by organizing your relationships. Both of these seem to be inseparable.

Chapter 3: Why It Is Important To Set Some Goals

"Perhaps that's why we seem to want everything when we are so close to wanting it all."

Sylvia Plat

Prior to decluttering or turning your life around, minimalism can be applied in your everyday life.

Our culture is very ambitious and encourages us all to set high goals. While we are encouraged to launch the next billion dollar startup, we also need to maintain a full schedule that includes travel, social events, and 100 books per annum. Society expects of us to do everything at once.

These goals emphasize being productive and busy over focusing on the important things. We become too caught up with our daily tasks and lose sight of the important things.

However, beneath all the hustle and bustle, you'll discover people who aren't certain what they want. Millions of people live their daily lives doing what they think is right and not what it is they love. If you feel that way, you're not alone.

This chapter is an invitation to stop and take a deep breath. What do YOU want from life? Minimalism is a way to achieve what you want. However, it's only possible if your goals are clear.

Without some goals, you're guaranteed to fail...

You can't have minimalism if your goals aren't clear. You will always be moving in the wrong direction and end up unhappy. You will get the most enjoyment out of minimalism if your goal is to live a life that you love.

It can be hard to make decisions about any major life decision without having clear goals. For example, you cannot decide whether to move across America with your boyfriend if it isn't clear what your goals are for your relationship. If you don't have the information to help you make a decision on which job offer or job, it will be difficult for your relationship to work out which one is best.

But this does not mean that your goal will never change. People who keep growing every year will find that their objectives change over time. Without a goal, it's impossible to grow towards it. It means that even the most energetic person, change can be difficult, slow, or unpredictable.

It's more effective to have a goal, to make some progress, then to sit around and wait for a plan. Being able to make progress increases your self-esteem. And you might find that the progress you have made toward your old goal will help you achieve your new goal.

But goals do not mean you should be rigid or strict in your life choices. There are many ways to change your mind. Some people move in to live with their partners before they get married. Some people have a kid before getting married. Some people travel the world for many years before finally settling down. For these changes to take place, however, you must be doing something.

Don't panic if it seems like you're drifting along in life. Minimalism will help set some goals. A bonus is that you will be more likely than ever to keep your eyes on those goals, and not lose heart. It doesn't matter what goal your start with; as long the list isn't too long, it doesn't matter.

Even though your best intentions sound realistic now, you still have plenty of potential for growth. Setting a goal to become a bestselling author is possible. Start by writing your first blog post. You could set a goal to run a full marathon and begin by walking around your neighborhood. It is possible to have many small goals, which will give you lots of opportunities to feel great about your accomplishments.

The best goals can also be their reward. You enjoy the journey and the goal. Writing blog posts is something you enjoy, as well as running at the track. This is something I won't have to tell you, but if your journey isn't enjoyable, you won't make it to the end.

All of this means that you can start anywhere you want. If you feel that writing a novel would be enjoyable, it might be worthwhile. It might be an option to go vegan if animal cruelty has been a cause close to your heart. They are yours. You decide.

But, even if your goals are inflexible, you're still bound to fail

Some recommend that you make concrete plans to reach your goals. This is a more detailed way to think of goals. The details of a plan can be complicated to track and lead to problems. This level of unreliable complexity is what the minimalist strives to avoid.

This type of planning doesn't work with many people and it certainly does not work well for me. I can't even count the times I have made daily-by-day plans and time-blocked calendar-blocked scheduling. According to productivity gurus "if it'snt on your agenda, it won't occur!" I find that things don't ever happen even though they are on my calendar. It takes me days to forget what my original plan was when I create detailed plans about how and what I will accomplish.

In the end, I was able to pursue my goals by letting go of rigid expectations and deciding how to attain them. Restricting your life to a certain schedule can hinder you from achieving what you want. You may be closing your eyes to possible possibilities. This is known in Zen as "too little willful will."

Zen talks about the issue of 'too little willful will.' This basically refers to trying too hard, being too intent. Real breakthroughs occur when you aren't as controlling and when your let go.

Ryan Holiday, One Little Decision Changed Everything in My Career

Exercising is difficult for many people because of their willful attitude. People believe they must exercise a certain time and in a particular manner, but end up never exercising as they can't meet their high standards.

Writing is the same. People have a tendency to think their writing must be a certain length.

Being flexible about your goals is what makes breakout successes possible. People who are successful have a clear goal and are willing to work hard to reach it. However, they also remain flexible when it comes to how and when they will achieve their goals. They are able to work hard and seize opportunities offered by others.

Why Successful People have Fewer Goals than Others

Minimalism is based on the fundamental principle that less stuff makes it easier to appreciate everything. The more you try to do things, the less likely you are to achieve your goals. The most successful people do not set too many goals.

Particularly for me, setting too high goals is a recipe for failure. Imagine that I have more than a handful items on my task list. I might find it overwhelming to see my to-dos and then I avoid them altogether in favor of completing a less important task. When I let myself go of the less important tasks, I'm able to get my most crucial jobs done.

Society expects us have many goals. We view ambitious people as ambitious. The more ambitious someone is, then the more they plan. Teachers, parents and bosses are critical of people who have only a few achievable goals. It doesn't matter if you don't achieve your goals. It's more beneficial to have a smaller number of achievable goals than to have many goals you don't know will ever be achieved.

The reality is that it's easy to make a list of goals for oneself, and you can't blame society. If you are looking for pictures that inspire you, Instagram is the best place to look. Combining Pinterest with Instagram creates an extremely dangerous combination. With platforms like this, it is easy to achieve a million-and-one goals for yourself. "That girl has a beautiful style!" I want to be like that." "I wish mine looked as beautiful as the model in this photograph." There are moments when it seems like the grass is always greener. But, it's unrealistic to allow these to influence our priorities.

Do not let your failures stop you from achieving these goals. It's okay to only have a few plans. Remind yourself that it is okay to pick a few.

It isn't that we shouldn't set goals. However, we will only benefit from setting goals that are consistent with our life purpose. Even though you may get a small benefit from setting goals for non-life purpose goals, the benefits are negligible compared to the joy and satisfaction that you get when you accomplish a goal that aligns closely with your purpose.

You can let go of the goal-shopping bandwagon by deciding to stop browsing Pinterest and instead focus on something more productive: your minimalism quest.

Select 5 Great Goals to Motivate You for Years

You only have five years to achieve the things you dream of. These could be things you really want, things you have to learn, skills you want, knowledge you need, or other interests.

It is likely that you already have a mental note like this somewhere in the brain. Perhaps you are a doctor or have always wanted to travel to every nation on the planet. These are not things to put on the back burner. They should be front-and-center. Then, you will be able to start actively looking for them.

If you are unable to help but to set twenty or 30 goals, select the most important five today and let the rest go. Once you have completed some of your existing goals, you can move on to your longer-term list of options and select something else. If you try and prioritize everything at once, it won't work. You can decide to defer some of your goals while you work on other things.

Sometimes it is a great idea to try things you aren't sure of. You might be surprised to discover that you can achieve more than what you imagined. Bo Burnham was a comedian and became internationally famous after uploading YouTube videos as an adolescent. He didn't know he would achieve that level of success but he did. The same could happen for you.

If all else fails consider learning a completely new language, listening to music, reading about the lives of people who have inspired you, and/or learning a new song. Add something completely new to your life if you feel stuck.

Your life can be precious and short. Get what you want now. You never know when it will be. It could be today, at 95, or in the future. Many people make the omission of what they really love and put it off for another day. When they reach the end their lives, they wish they could go back. Seneca spoke thousands of year ago that "Life can be long if we know how to make it work."

This is an opportunity to be kind to yourself. You don't have to get discouraged for not reaching all the items on your list of thirty or more. Yes, you may die tomorrow, but you can't help it if you do. You're expecting too many things from yourself. Start with a few main points, then move on.

Do not fall into the Overthinking trap

Don't get too involved in this. This exercise can be very personal. This exercise is highly personal. The best choices for one person might be disastrous for another. The list of one person may look great, but the list of another person will be different. This is where you need your gut to guide you. If you have the opportunity, this is your chance to get a broad idea of what interests you in your life.

If you find the term "goals" too daunting, consider using "passions." Many people believe that the word goal implies time limits and a sense if urgency. A goal of $1,000,000 in income by 30 may be seen as more of a burden that an aspiration. You either achieve it or you don't. There is no "in-between".

Passion isn't subject to any external pressure. Your passion will be what it is. You have the right to live your passion for as long as you want.

My list is...

To live to the fullest as a healthy senior.

To travel slowly, but often.

To achieve financial independence.

To improve critical thinking skills.

To have a deeply fulfilling marriage.

As you read this book you will be asked again and again whether it supports you in your goals. You will get the life you desire. Don't miss this part.

Chapter 4: Minimalism And Clutter

The very word minimalism might conjure up a vivid image of a light-flooded, clean room with minimal furniture. You will have a different experience with minimalism depending on your personal taste.

Minimalism is about making room for the most important parts of your life. It is possible to make more space in your life and find happiness and meaning by getting rid off unnecessary stuff. Minimalism allows for you to focus on the important things in life, such as love, relationships and positive experiences.

Most people prefer a clean and clutter-free home. More space and less visual distractions can lead to calmness, serenity, peace of thoughts, and calmness. At least in theory, it is not difficult to lead a minimalist lifestyle. There are just two steps to simplify your life: identifying and eliminating clutter. This is only a part of it all. Even though the beginning can seem daunting, it's not difficult to get there. It gets easier as you go along. It is possible to live a more uncluttered life and you will not want to go back.

Before you can identify clutter, it is important to first consider your whys. Why do you want less clutter? There must have been a reason why you chose this book.

Perhaps you are overwhelmed at the amount of stuff you have built up over the years. Maybe you're looking to save money and get rid of your credit card debt. It may be necessary to move to a better place, with fewer possessions. This could be because you are trying to regain your time and stop caring about stuff you don't really need. Or maybe you care about protecting nature and want it to be less environmentally-friendly. If possible, think about your reasons and make a list. Next, imagine yourself living in a decluttered home or enjoying the activities you dream of. How does your environment look to you? How do they make you feel? It's unnecessary clutter that only hinders your future self vision. William Morris said that minimalism is the best way to live. "Have nothing inside your house that you don't believe to be useful or beautiful." Every person has their own definitions of the terms useful and beautiful. If you think about all the stuff you've accumulated over the years you may conclude that everything is either useful, useful someday, or beautiful. It wouldn't be there if it weren't. When you take the same objects from the perspective point of time their beauty and usefulness begin to diminish. Every material possession you own takes time. It takes your life away from you. It is time that you cannot get back. Time you could have spent better. Before you bring it into you life, a material object can eat up your time. It occupies your thoughts by making you think, reading reviews, comparing prices, searching for alternatives and choosing what is best for you. In order to be able to afford the item and the space it takes up, you'll need more time. When you buy new material, you also make an implicit commitment to cleaning, organizing, repairing, replacing, selling or other disposal of the item. The time you spend in an unorganized environment can lead to a depressing mood.

Our perceptions of the world around us are influenced by our physical surroundings. They try to make us feel inadequate and unfulfilled. We strive for the illusion of completeness, which we can only achieve by acquiring more material possessions. We are constantly comparing ourselves with others. However, comparison is not a winning strategy. There will always people with more of what you value or the things that you wish for. It's important to understand and love yourself for who you are. It doesn't make you better than other people, just being yourself is sufficient. Happiness can only come from within. Without being aware, most people try to heal deep emotional wounds through accumulation. You will never be able to fill your heart with material possessions. The superficiality of your consumption will soon fade away, but you will quickly realize the gaping wound that lies beneath it is still there. The inevitable end of life is not when we'll be wishing we could have bought more stuff, like a big house, an expensive car, or a widescreen TV. Most likely, however, we would be reflecting back on our lives and the things we did and didn't do. The happier we live, the sooner we can reflect on our values.

Lifestyle benefits that are minimalist

Minimalist living can transform your life. There are many benefits to minimalism. In my opinion, there is no drawback to only keeping what you use. Following is a quick list of the many wonderful benefits you can get by living a minimalist lifestyle.

You can do it more often

This is an important benefit. This is what I consider the greatest advantage to being minimalist. It's priceless to have more time for what matters. You might feel overwhelmed and lack the time to clean up your home. Perhaps you would like to, but don't know how. It is more difficult to achieve this goal if you have more things over the years. But it is possible to begin slowly. Slower is always better than none at all. A set time block each day for decluttering, and make sure you stick to it. This time slot is yours to declutter. Decluttering can make your life easier and will bring you great rewards. When your home and life are clutter-free, you'll be amazed at the positive changes that will occur in your life.

More money

You will be able spend more money on worthwhile causes and meaningful things.

It takes less space to live in.

Reduced square footage is possible when you eliminate clutter. It is simpler to maintain a smaller home and it is also less expensive. You can move to a higher-end location with fewer possessions.

Easier cleaning

If you are anything like mine, you likely hate cleaning. I enjoy a clean place, but I don't enjoy cleaning. I view cleaning as a means of an end, a real chore and something that I do not enjoy. The sooner it is over, the better.

Quality products

Minimalism isn't the same as deprivation or thriftiness. It's possible to save money by not buying the things you don't want.

Less stress

Stress is an all-pervasive word in modern culture. Clutter creates stress. We feel anxious and down when we are confronted with clutter. A ban on clutter in our homes is good for our mental health. You can do a simple exercise. Consider taking pictures of your kitchen in different situations. The first picture shows random things covering your counters and dining tables. In the second case, dirty dishes pile up in the kitchen sink. In the second situation, the kitchen is clean, with no dishes on the sink. Compare both digital and mental images. Which do you prefer? In your kitchen or in a different setting? It most likely isn't the latter. Relaxing in your own home can make life easier.

Be more productive

Reduced visual distractions, fewer to do lists in the back of your head or cluttering up the phone app or notebook will allow you to focus more on the task and get it done faster.

Set an example for your kids

Children will follow our values and behaviors. If we are able to show them that happiness is not equal to material possessions, they will be more responsible citizens in the future.

Improved relationships

Uncluttered living allows us to be more present with those we love. This, in turn, can have a positive effect upon our relationship.

More freedom

You have more freedom when you own less stuff. Freedom to pursue the hobbies we enjoy with fewer distractions and to move our household from one location to another.

Our loved ones will feel less pain after our death

Our lives will end, no matter how hard we try not to think about it. Each person will experience death at some time. We don't wish to make our loved ones feel worse by adding to their emotional suffering by making our household messy and cluttered.

The environment is good

As a kid, our house overlooked a small natural reserve. If I had to describe the sound of the nights back in those warm times of the years with just one word, it would be magical. The moonlit tree leaves rustled in the light summer breeze, their sounds blending with the songs from crickets and frogs creating an extraordinary symphony. Myriad sparkling stars lit up the velvety sky. There were many things to do in those days: running among lush green grass and chasing butterflies; wondering at the tiny scales of limber geckos. Nature was alive with life and exquisite beauty. That was 30 years ago. This is not the way it looks today. And I don't know what it will look like 30 years from now. Today I find that my home town has very few wildflowers. There is no crickets, frogs, or geckos. And there are no butterflies. Even though there are only a few dim stars at nights, they seem much higher up than they used to. I can't help but feel devastated by the recklessness of our human lifestyles and how they irreversibly damage our planet.

Every person has a personal reason to want less stuff. Whatever your motivations, a minimalist lifestyle will give you more space to follow your dreams and make your life more enjoyable. Minimalist living is more than reducing your possessions down to the essentials. Minimalist living encompasses more than this. Minimalism is a universal principle, which can be applied in any aspect of your lives.

Chapter 5: Arranging And De-Cluttering Laundry And Washroom

This assignment applies regardless if your washer and dryer are located in a devoted or carport. (My washer/dryer are my very own guest washroom!) It is incredible to see how quickly we can build up a mess. The washer and dryer have level surfaces. It is not difficult to place things over them, especially if the washer does not have a top-stacked clothes washer which requires you to lift the cover every time you wash something. However, it is unlikely that you will keep much stuff on these surfaces. Instead, over the course the Challenge, you will make room for clothing supplies to be stored nearby but not on the washer/dryer. These could be stored on a rack, in the cupboard, or in clothing caddies between machines.

The pantry is not able to achieve its grandiose goals of tidiness or request. Torn socks and missing button shirts are all mixed with cleansers bottles, dirty and clean garments, and dryer sheet. You don't need to worry: There are many ways to create a space that is slimmest possible with these tips and hacks.

So-Smart Laundry Room Storage Solutions

1. Level is Where it's at

Clean clothing can be one thing, while collapsed clothing can be another. Deborah J. Cabral, a certified proficient coordinator, says, "What people forget is the taking of part." It can end up on the stairs and in a box. Cabral encourages you to avoid stackable equipments for front-stacking the alternatives one next to another; at that point top both using a small overlay ledge for an overlapped spot.

2. Start with a Schedule

The best and most luxurious pantry on Earth won't work. Instead, experts suggest you think about how to organize your calendar. Cabral takes care of her clothes every day. Her children will have to take care of their clothing. She suggests that she sits down with her family to discuss their needs and decide what will work best for them. For example, sports gear may need to be washed twice a week on Tuesday and Friday. Kathy Jenkins has established days to wash sheets and towels. The benefits are double. One, the particular washday takes away the guilt that comes with neglecting to clean those things. She never has to fuss about taking care of sheets or towels.

3. Where is the real clutter?

The clothing territory is often a small area of a mudroom or storeroom. As such, it can become a vault to store single socks. However, it can also hold a lot other odd stuff (additional lights, travel ornaments) for which there is no additional space. Jenkins said, "It is this place where, on the off possibility that we don't know where something has to go, it gets put inside the pantry." Your pantry will soon become a dismal mess if you allow all of these things to accumulate. Instead, search for real homes for your items with dedicated, named, readily available compartments.

4. What to do about those missing socks?

There's a certain trust in the possibility that the missing socks will return, even if you have to search constantly for them. Is this feasible? Designate a section to hold socks (without mates) and a sequence of events to facilitate hurling. Mindy Godding, proficient coordinator, recommends another suggestion: You can toss single socks into the right closet space. She said, "At the point you realize where they are when or if it is their mates." Then again, give each relative an extra work bag to hold dirty socks. Sets are seldom isolated in a perfect world. Keep a few basic tools, like scissors, string and needles, in your pantry to fix those stitches.

5. Try not to Be a Scrooge in the Basket

Godding encourages you to use clothes crates in every washroom. Cabral suggests families with kids use shading coded clothing carriers. One is for lights, the other for darks. Loads and loads of clothing containers in different places discourage family members from throwing dirty clothes on the kitchen floor or in the bathroom.

6.Agree with a Friend

Godding treasures her rolled clothing sorter. It can be divided into three separate compartments for light, dark and bright hues. She recommends that you invest your time and resources in something that helps keep clothing off of the floor, regardless of how organized you are. She says she's seen pantries flooded with clothes and linens that cover the floor. These mayhems require that clean items are washed numerous times in order to ensure they remain spotless. Jenkins suggests keeping the sorter and apparatuses as close to the source as possible. "I'm not very good with clothes, but if the white compartment in my sorter is full, then I realize I need a bunch.

Start Small

Small loads, especially for clothing with limited space, can lessen the impact of the overwhelming clothing clutter that can lead to chaos. Godding comments, "I believe in doing small loads more often than one clothing day." Additionally, less burdens are easier and quicker to manage.

8. To Dry It Out Or Not

Balance garments before drying can prevent contracting, blurring, or other damage caused by heat. Accordion-style drying shelves can be space-savers as well as mess cutters. They are designed to be used when they aren't in use and can pull out easily for drying fragile items. Jenkins recommends that you skim the wooden ones in order to avoid any danger of form.

9. Know Your Properties

Many clothing "rooms", while they may appear to be storage, are actually closets. Wardrobes can often have doors. It's not a lot of people who use that land. To increase crawling for dryer sheets, or other clothing necessities, you can install a thin stockpiling piece that screws into the entryway. Fill the void divider with snares to make the dryer appear amazing, eliminating the need to press.

In the event that you cannot install a cupboard to cover your machines, use racks that are extremely well-constructed and connect at the rear of your washer or dryer. Tossing stuff over the apparatus can result in chaos. This arrangement holds everything up to the sky. If you do not have a desk, place similar supplies, like color removers, in a single compartment. This makes it simple to pick up, use, and then set aside.

10. Time it Out

Inability to arrange causes chaos. Neglecting to arrange clothes can lead to inefficiency. The average pile of clothing takes me five mins to crease. Jenkins says it takes much less than most people would think. Godding advises that you try to use clocks in order to remove the burdens of laundry and drying.

11. It Could Not Be Your Laundry Room's Fault

The fault could not lie with your pantry if you constantly go through your clothing bag in search of something to wear. This is typically a sign of a nonfunctional or swarmed drawer or storage space. Because the person is wearing garments right now, the crate contains garments that will no longer fit or are out of date. You can make a significant difference by decluttering your pantry as well as your wardrobe. "Great clothing frameworks increase the life expectancy of garments, and allow you to feel relaxed when getting dressed.

Chapter 6: Living A Minimalistic Life

Living minimalistically doesn't just mean decluttering your home and changing your buying habits. There are other ways to incorporate minimalistic living. These include selling your car and using public transportation, buying less furniture, and clearing digital clutter from your cellphone.

Your Home

You should ensure enough space in your new home for you, family members, and all your belongings. You might find there is more space in your house if you begin to organize and get rid off unnecessary items. Many people want their home to be more spacious and minimalist.

But for others, empty spaces can make them feel isolated. This is especially true for families who have built large homes for their growing family only to see their children go off to college and start their own lives. The empty space leaves them feeling lost. For them, it's easy to move down to a smaller house with the rooms they actually need.

It's possible to get a smaller house for yourself and the people you share it with and save money so you can spend that money on something you really desire. After decluttering most of my possessions, I was surprised at how little I actually needed in order to have a productive day.

Furniture

Once you have decluttered the house, you may discover furniture that is no longer needed or used. Your old furniture will be sold, and you'll have money left over to put in savings, buy new furniture, or get furniture of better quality.

In addition to buying high-quality furniture for your home, minimalist furniture is also available. A plain glass desk can replace an old, bulky or antique desk. Minimalist furniture places emphasis on functionality, and minimizes storage space.

You will be able to eliminate clutter from your home by using this type of furniture. This type furniture will give your home a clean and tidy look, which you can then decorate with ornaments, sentimental or other items. They fill up the space but don't make it too cluttered.

Transportation

Another way you can simplify you life that you may not have thought of is to choose the right type car. It is important to think about how frequently you use your car. If your vehicle is only used to transport you to work, the shop, and then back to home, you might consider buying a smaller, more efficient car, a scooter,, or even an electric bicycle. These forms of transportation can be cheaper to keep and maintain, require less gas to drive, and can be more sustainable.

If you have enough money and are interested in an electric car, you may also consider buying one. An electric vehicle runs on electricity, so it will need to be charged. This can save you gas and help reduce your carbon footprint. Even though an electric car offers many advantages, this is still an expensive purchase. You can make better decisions before buying something like this.

Public transport could be another option. While it takes some planning to ensure the right bus or train is taking you from one place to another, it can soon become part of your daily routine. You can hop on a train or bus and get to wherever you need to go. If you're careful, you may never need to buy another car.

Uber and other car-sharing services might be a better option if you don't have many ways to get around the city. Uber can be pricey, but it is convenient and quick if you do not travel that far.

You can find many other ways to travel without a car. It is crucial that you find a reliable and affordable way to travel, regardless of whether you plan to trade in your car to eliminate financial and other clutter.

Digital Clutter

The other large part of your lifestyle that you can clear out is your smartphone, tablet, laptop, or any other electronic device where you store photos and documents. Your stress levels and clutter can be reduced by getting rid of digital clutter from your devices, and reducing the amount you get from social media. These easy and quick changes can help you eliminate the clutter from your life so you can spend more time on the things you love.

It is possible to clear out digital clutter by scanning your inbox and unimportant emails. This is something I do every day.

Then I go through the emails that are most important and decide which ones should be deleted. If you don't feel like deleting your most important email, you can archive them. This will ensure that they do not go in your inbox but remain in the archived folder until you need them.

While you are busy deleting spam emails, it is a good idea to go through your email and click the unsubscribe link. Scroll to the bottom and you will find the button or link. You might also want to check your spam mailbox to see if there are any unsubscribed emails. These emails may also be removed from your spam folder to stop them coming through to you.

Once your emails are organized, you can create some folders to organize those emails that you have chosen to keep or ones you will get in the future. I have created the following folders. Drag my emails to each folder.

* Reply later. I respond immediately to emails that arrive. If they are not, they will be moved to the archive folder. I may receive more detailed emails that I need my attention. All these emails will go into the archive folder. They will then be dealt with later in day or when they are available for me to reply to. After I've replied to them, I will send them to the archives folder.

* Bank. I will keep all emails, statements and payment alerts from the bank in this folder. To keep it relevant and organized, I will remove this folder every 6-12 months.

* Car. Any emails I receive from the bank that finances my vehicle will be moved to this folder. I will also move any emails related to car insurance into this folder. I will check my emails for car financing every 6-12months. I will not delete emails related to car insurance until I have traded in the car. I will, however, delete the less important documents and keep the original contract that I signed at the car dealership.

* Contracts. I will keep all documents and emails pertaining to contractual agreements that I signed (e.g. phone contracts, lease agreements, etc.) in this folder. These emails will be kept as long my contract is valid and as long that I am renting the house where I'm staying.

* Medical. I will keep in this folder all emails from the hospital and doctors regarding payments, prescriptions or notifications. This folder will only be removed every 6-12months, after which I will pay any outstanding amounts.

* Tax. * Tax. I will keep all tax related information in this folder. These emails I will delete after I have filed taxes.

The downloads area is a common place that clutter builds up quickly on your PC. You do not have to worry if you remove downloaded files after using them. If you do not mind storing files for a longer time than you normally would, check the folder to verify what you have saved.

It's a good idea for you to take some time and look through all the files in your downloads directory at least once a week. This will depend on how often you download files. Once you have identified which files you don't use, you can remove them and move the files you do not need to into the right folders.

The easiest way to organize your files is by placing them within their own folders. People make hundreds of folders that contain every type of document or file that they download. This sounds good if you feel like you are able and confident to navigate through everything.

Sometimes you will need to go through the folders in your current system and simplify them. If you frequently place documents on your main desktop screen you may need to organize them into folders. This will help clear up any file clutter. An unorganized desktop screen can make you feel anxious.

My goal is to not place folders more than 2 or 3 levels deep when I work with folders. This makes it easy to track everything on my computer. To reduce confusion and to make it easier to find what you meant when creating a folder, you should keep your labelling as simple as you can. "Term 1 Project 3", is easier to recognize than "T1 P3".

Your folders can be arranged by priority, year, category, or any other method you like. I prefer to organize my documents by category. For instance, I might use folder names like Documents. This gives me a quick overview of what documents I have within each folder. If someone needs my computer, it is also easy to explain.

If you have many files and folders on your computer that you don't need, an external drive might be worth it. The external hard drive can hold all files and folders, but you can only keep those you use. This helps to reduce clutter and makes your computer more spacious for what you need.

Pictures stored on your computer, on an external hard disk, or in the Cloud can take up space that is better used for other documents. Regularly review your pictures and make sure to delete the ones you don't want.

If you're having trouble finding enough storage space, you can transfer your photos to the Cloud and delete them from any local device. You can also place your pictures onto an external hard-drive. So, even if your computer or phone is lost, you'll still be able to access your favorite photos.

Social media has dominated our lives. While it can be overwhelming to receive so many updates and stories daily from your friends, only half of those people you have friend requested or followed are true friends. This step can be adjusted based on your preferences. I prefer to keep people on the friend or following list if we are close friends or we speak often enough to make them my friends.

You can check your friends or following list on a regular basis and remove people you don't know, or who aren't adding any value to the life of your family. You can also remove anyone who posts negative or disagreeable updates to your newsfeed. You should do the same thing for all your contacts.

It's a good idea while going through your contact list on your phone to review which apps you use. To declutter your phone and free up space for the important things, you can remove any apps you haven't used in a while. If you discover that you still need the application, you can then install it again. You should do this at minimum once a week for any app that you haven't used.

Chapter 7: How Can You Be One?

There is always an expense to pay. Each change in life brings with it a lesson. I can confidently say that you will learn from any challenge. The universe trusts that you will learn and that it will never stop you from living your life.

It is difficult for us to let go our possessions and people. Isn't it? It is this lesson that will help you become a minimalist. You don't need to be afraid. There are simpler ways to make this a habit. But this will help you not only become a minimalist but also a better human being, which is what life is all about. Be a better version of yourself and simplify your life. These qualities will stick with you as long as you work hard at Letting Go. This can be done by intellectualizing, feeling it internally and then putting it into motion. If you have ever reflected on your life while reading, then you are likely to have realized the logic of becoming a minimalist.

What does Letting Go really imply? It is okay to let go of someone or something. If we become attached to something or people and it becomes difficult to live and imagine our life without them, that is a sign it is time to let go. This aspect of our lives isn't adding value if we fully understand it. But is it really?

You need to be prepared for changes in your life.

That is the moment when we really let go. It is a process that leads to divine power.

What if you need it

What percentage of you had planned to clean out your wardrobe? How many felt that I would keep some things just in case. I have many of these things in my house, which my family isn't even aware of. They don't add any value, and I know many of you reading this book would agree.

The fear of not having enough or FOMO (fear about missing out), wat is it and so forth, are the main reasons we accumulate. We accumulate many things because we fear not having enough, FOMO (fear of missing out), wat if I need it and so on. How many times have you bought clothes without the tags intact? Or kept a bottle or two of alcohol in your closet for an event that never happened. Or kept a luxury car with no parking because it was too expensive, not used every day, or jewelry that has lost its value. Or the wedding gown you bought for thousands of rupees but have never worn again. If you answered "yes" to any of these scenarios, or have you ever been in a similar circumstance in your own life, then you are probably living in the What if State and not using your resources properly.

Do you think you might have accumulated these possessions because you did not need them but want them? An awareness problem exists where there is not enough distinction between artificial happiness, and real happiness. You may have felt that you want something urgently, but when you do get it, the excitement is different.

This happens because your search for something you don't need or adds value to life was unsuccessful. Your decision was a compensatory to your feelings and you will soon realize that LIFE is what you are looking for.

And sometimes, we start comparing ourselves with others and start accumulating negative thoughts, emotions and then compensating by accumulating in concrete of things.

Few days ago. I actually went shopping along with my friend. I saw him purchasing jackets. I asked him to clarify if he actually needed all of them. He said that I could use it if I needed it. I might go to a function or party next year. But all purchases were made with the assumption of what if. Discounts and sales can also be reasons we accumulate. And he did just that and has not touched the jackets for months.

In the memories

This is primarily related to the people around us. While it may seem harsh to some people, it is a perspective that I have and would like you to see. I have had many experiences throughout my life that show me that I no longer attach to material things. I have worked on my attachment to things related to others, and continue to do so. It's not something that you can learn immediately. When you see the benefits to learning from your past, it will be like a blessing.

Today's digital world is full of information and digitization. As a way to keep the memories alive, take a photograph. This is just a suggestion and perspective that I have gained from personal experience. You can give this stuff to someone else. We end up accumulating the stuff with us. Here is an example. My grandmother, who died 20 years ago, was my mother. My grandmother passed away 20 years ago. In her memory, my father took a table from her house and bought two chairs. That particular piece of furniture has been kept in the house, despite it taking up space and taking up space. However, we have more things to keep it there which aren't used for months or even years.

A lack of...

Chapter 8: Why Do We Clutter Our Lives?

Have you ever sat down to think about the reasons your life is so miserable? The answer to this question for many would be "No, you don't know why." They never think the reason their home isn't big enough to fit all their belongings is due to clutter. They believe the loft or house they live in is too small, and that they need to move into a larger home.

However, you can rest and take a look at it briefly. You are not putting your life at risk. I'm sure you are reading this book to learn more about the moderate way to live. Because the first step is to clean out our lives, we want the underlying cause to be identified so we don't continue to repeat the cycle.

Take this as an example:

You were looking for data on...suppose...the ideal weight loss diet. Every weight reduction blog you come across makes promises about simple weight reduction strategies. You enjoy all you are seeing so much that you want to receive their email updates to keep you informed about future weight reduction information. Does this sound like something you did once? Perhaps not for weight-reduction plans, but for something entirely different. This is the first reason why we mess with our lives.

Fear of Missing it (FOMO).

You preferred the online journals with more detailed information. However, if the habit is to subscribing to random websites without thinking about it, then you will be inundated with junk emails and your email will become almost frightening. However, we are not in the habit of doing this as we don't want anyone to miss out. We would rather not feel regret that maybe something did not work out, based on the crucial data we have missed.

Interestingly, FOMO isn't restricted to email pamphlets. It is common in nearly all areas of our life. Let's take for example web-based communication: How often did you decide to deactivate your Facebook account? You know how much energy you have there and you don't want it to be reactivated the next morning.

It is absolutely impossible to keep track of everything on the internet or web-based media. Yet, we can still use the internet for our personal lives and work. Once you accept that you won't be able to keep up with everything no matter how much you try, then you can stop trying to make sense of your existence. To become a minimalist, you have to face the fear of missing an opportunity.

Let's take another example: After shopping for food, you get home with nylon bags. So what do you do? You either put them in the trash/recycling bin immediately or you tuck them away. This is why clutter is so common in our lives.

They Might be Needed Later

This entire cleaning thing requires a huge mental perspective. You will probably not have to use those nylon sacks. This is evident by the fact your kitchen is full of nylon sacks that have been discarded. This is why we keep doing it. What's the point of bringing stuff into our homes when we are aware that we might never need them? Why do we put off getting rid of unnecessary items?

These are the questions that you ask to determine the best option for your home. A sincere response to this inquiry and the willingness and discipline to make the best choice will help you get on a different track to achieve more with your time. Marie Kondo offers a model in her book, The Life-

Changing Magistral Magic of Tidying Up: How to Declutter and Organize Your Life.

I vividly recall a time when I illustrated to a CEO the best way for him to clean his office. His bookshelves were stuffed full of titles that sound difficult, but which you would expect a company chief to read.

Drucker and Carnegie are just a few examples. It was like walking into an actual book shop. I knew what I was seeing when I saw his array. After being sufficiently certain, he started to arrange them. He piled an endless series of books onto "all his" piles, reporting that they were uninitiated. He was actually carrying fifty volumes and barely had made an imprint on the first. When I asked why they were kept, he gave me the most convincing answer from my list of plausible answers: "Since that I should peruse them at some stage." Although I can personally see the dangers in this, I don't believe that "at some point", ever comes.

Yes, there is some deception. It never happens.

Yet another motivating factor is at work in why we ruin our lives.

I can always bring it back later

How many times are you guilty of putting things where they don't belong in your home in the hope that later they will be in their proper place? Reason: Your life is too busy. How often are you unable to make the right decision? This is probably the best reason for messing around at home and in work. You remove a document from a cabinet. But rather than returning it back to the cabinet once you are done with it and keep control of it, you place the document on the table with the intention of returning the item later. It takes just 2 minutes to return a document to the cabinet. You don't need any investment to do the right task.

This is what we do in the home. It was after I finished drying my body in the shower that

I remembered how I used to get my body cream from the dresser. Yet, I would not set it back at all. For the love and honor of all that is holy and pure, the table is always there. In fact, I might have placed it back exactly where it was from. However, this is how I see it now. This is because I took time to question myself and became deliberate about decluttering and enjoying the benefits and simplicity of a minimalist lifestyle.

You don't need a receipt to return your item. You have created a mess and will need to clean it up later. Your hair will be more messy the longer you keep it.

The more actual space you have, then your psyche is likely to be confused.

The joy of owning

If a few women are particularly conscious of their looks, they may purchase another dress. Then they will put on the dress normally and then take a look at themselves in the mirror. They feel like they are the proud owner of this dress.

When buying a new vehicle, you'll need to constantly inspect it and feel it. They may even refer to the new vehicle as their "child". Owning stuff gives you some satisfaction. Additional remedial measures include buying new stuff. A few people cover up their troubles by shopping for new items or indulgently. Being able to see their stuff brings them joy. This is one more reason why people can mess up their lives. They need to work hard and put effort into resolving problems each day.

Once the next big thing goes public, and you start seeing celebrities using it, you must also buy it. Another reason to consume it is the pleasure of claiming it and being among the incident individuals.

There is satisfaction in having new things. But there is more joy in living well. Do not be a slave of things, but rather become an expert. There are a few things that you don't need even though you will use them. It is a good idea to lease any thing you can find for rent, especially if it is something that you use only once per year. You don't need it if you only use it occasionally.

Chapter 9: Why Do We Clutter Our Lives?

Have you ever sat down to think about the reasons your life is so miserable? The answer to this question for many would be "No, you don't know why." This is because they never think the reason their home is too small to accommodate all of their belongings is due to clutter. They feel the house or loft is too small for them so they want a bigger house.

However, you can rest and contemplate it briefly. You are not wasting your time. I'm sure you're reading this book to learn more about the moderate way to live. Because the first step is to clean out our lives, we want the underlying cause to be identified so that we don't continue to repeat the cycle.

Consider this scenario.

You were looking for information on... suppose... the ideal weight loss diet. Each weight loss blog you come across has tempting comments about easy weight management plans. You like everything you are seeing and so you have decided to sign up for their email updates to ensure that you do not miss out on future information about weight reduction. This sounds like something you may have done once before. Maybe not for weight-reduction plans, but for something entirely different. That brings us to our primary point:

Fear of Missing it (FOMO).

You might have preferred those online journals that were focused on getting you more information. However, if you have a habit of subscribing to random websites, you will be inundated with random junk mail from those sites. It will almost become terrifying to open these emails. However, we are not in the habit of doing this as we do not want any information to go unanswered. We would rather not feel regret that maybe something did not work out, based on the crucial data we have missed.

Interestingly, FOMO isn't restricted to email pamphlets. It is common in nearly all aspects our lives. Let's take for example web-based communication: How often did you decide to deactivate your Facebook account? You know how much energy you have there and you don't want it to be reactivated the next morning.

It is almost impossible for us to keep track of everything on the web or web-based media. Yet, we can still use the internet to help our personal lives and work. Once you accept that you won't be able to keep up with everything no matter what, you will stop trying. To become a minimalist, you have to face the fear of missing an opportunity.

Let's take another example: After shopping for food, you get home with nylon bags that you need to throw away. So what do you do? You either put them in the trash/recycling container immediately or you tuck them away. This is why clutter can be so destructive to our lives.

They Might Be Needed Later

This entire cleaning thing requires a huge mental perspective. It is unlikely that you will ever require nylon bags. This is obvious because you can see your kitchen cluttered with nylon bags you've never used. This is why we keep doing this. What's the point of bringing stuff into our homes when we are aware that they might not be used? Why do we put off getting rid of unnecessary items?

These are the questions that you ask to determine the best solution for keeping your belongings in your home. A sincere response to this inquiry and the willingness and discipline to make the best choice will help you get on a different track to achieve more with your time. Marie Kondo offers a model in her book, The Life-Changing Magistral Magic of Tidying Up: How to Declutter and Organize Your Life.

I vividly recall a time when I was illustrating a CEO how to clean his office. His bookshelves were stuffed full of titles that sound difficult, like classics by authors.

Drucker and Carnegie are just a few examples. It felt almost like walking into an actual bookshop. I knew what I was seeing when I first saw the assortment. After being sufficiently certain, he began to arrange them. He piled an interminable number of books on each pile, reporting that they were all uninitiated. When he was done, he had fifty volumes. The first edition had seen very little use. When I asked him to explain why he kept them for so long, he responded with one of my most convincing answers: "Since, I should peruse this at some stage." Although I have personal experience that I can see you right now, it is possible that "at some point" never arrives.

Yes, there is some deception. It never comes.

There is another reason our lives get messed up, and most people are to blame.

It's always possible to put it back later

How many times are you guilty of placing things in places they don't belong? Then again, what about putting them in their best place so that you can put them back where they belong. Reason: Your life is too busy. How often are you unable to make the right decision? This is probably the best reason for messing around at home and in work. You remove a document from a cabinet. But rather than returning it when you are done using it and keeping control of it, you place the document on the table with the intention of returning the item later. This is fun because it would only take 2 minutes to return the paper to the cabinet. It doesn't require any investment to do the right task.

This is what we do in the home. It was after I finished drying my body in the shower that I remembered how I would grab the body cream and place it on the dressing room table. Yet, I didn't want to move it from its current position. I am grateful for the table and may have placed it back right where I took it. However, this is how I see it now. This is because I have taken the initiative to declutter my life and enjoy the minimalist lifestyle.

You don't have a responsibility to return the item you purchased when you receive it. If you stick your antiperspirant, hairbrush, or body cream in an unacceptable place, you are creating a mess. Your hair will be more disorganized the longer you keep it.

The more actual space you have, your psyche is likely to be confused. There is most definitely a relationship, and you should always remember it.

The joy of ownership

If a few women are particularly conscious of how they look, they may buy another dress. They feel great about being the proud owner of their dress.

It is vital that you inspect and feel the vehicle before buying a new vehicle. They may even refer to the new vehicle as their "child". Owning stuff gives you some satisfaction. Additional remedial measures include buying new stuff. Some people cover up their troubles by buying new or indulgent items. Being able to see their stuff brings them joy. This is one more reason why people can mess up their lives. They need to work hard and put effort into resolving problems each day.

Once the next big thing goes public, and you start seeing celebrities using it, you must also buy it. Another reason to consume it is the pleasure of claiming it and having a spot among the incident individuals.

There is satisfaction in having new things. But there is more joy in living well. Do not be a captive to these things, but rather become an expert. There are some things you don't need even though they may be necessary. It is advisable to lease any equipment that you can obtain for rent, particularly if it is something you use only once per month. You don't have the right to keep it if it isn't something you use often.

Chapter 10: Minimalist Home Decorating

Minimalism doesn't have to mean living in an apartment. You can make your home look as beautiful and elegant as you want without the need to have elaborate furniture. Let's examine how to decorate your home with minimalist decor tips.

Restrained colors are best - Use neutrals, almost-white colours, pastels, as well white to color your walls. You can choose bright colors in smaller spaces to emphasize a particular part of the house.

It is easy to accentuate pastels and neutral shades by using bright colors in small spaces. Another benefit of neutrals like beige, pastels, is that they create a feeling of well-lit rooms even when there's no artificial lighting. A white marble dining table is another way to add neutrals to your home decor.

Maximize the power and beauty of empty space. Minimalism is more than keeping your home uncluttered. Minimalism can be described as the art of combining space with items in a stylish and beautiful way.

This combination should be achieved seamlessly without objects becoming distracting. Your essential decor items and family decor will be prominent in such environments, drawing attention to the observer's eyes without being distracting.

Use accents to add color and decoration - This is a reminder of what I said earlier. A minimalist home doesn't have to be empty of colors and decorations. It is just more minimalist than a home that isn't minimalist. Your decorations should be accentuated in the background with subtlety.

A colorful, vibrant painting on a wall of neutral colors enhances its beauty and makes it stand out from the rest. If your home is over-decorated, your guests will feel overwhelmed. This can be a negative sign that your home is not welcoming and pleasant.

Each area should have a focal point, with the decorations and colors. Even subtle background shades can give the picture an elegant minimalism.

You don't have only one way to decorate your house. The white kitchen cabinets are open and airy, with no handles. The no-handles cabinet is flat, creating a seamless beauty. The pastels and the flat surfaces are the main focus.

Keep non-essentials out of reach in cabinets. Make sure you clear spaces such as countertops, etc. Make sure you only have the essentials. All other items must have their own designated space in cabinets, drawers, storage units, or elsewhere in your home.

This is an example of what your kitchen countertop should look like:

* The hob, or the gas stove

* The microwave and oven

Apart from the two above, you might have one or two other essential work items, such knives neatly organized in a tray, a small vase of fresh flower arrangements, and perhaps a dish or two to give the space the appearance of a real kitchen. All other kitchen elements should be kept in cabinets. A beautiful kitchen is one with a clean, organized, and uncluttered layout.

Try out different textures and colors for your furnishings. This includes curtains, upholstery, and fabric. You can also reflect minimalism by using pastel shades on the walls. Pastel colours on the walls, and bright red curtains for the large windows could detract from the idea of minimalism. Red curtains aren't necessarily a no-no for minimalism. It's only that bright colors shouldn't be used in excess.

A splash of pink on your sofa cushions, or a bold painting on the wall can bring life and character to your home's decor. A little color can be a great accent to a neutral or pastel-toned backdrop.

Keep your eyes on the floors and windows. Simple windows can also be used as decoration. Curtains do not always need to be present in every room. Instead, let natural sunlight infiltrate your home and enhance its minimalist aesthetic.

If privacy is a must, use the smallest curtain material possible to let in natural light. Shutter curtains, which are almost as minimalist as it gets, can be used for your living space's windows.

Wooden floors provide warmth and a minimalist look to the space. They are also easy to maintain. The color of the wooden flooring can make or destroy the decor in a room. You should make wise choices.

Enjoy the beauty of pattern - Checked and striped or color coordinated patterns can increase the beauty, elegance, and beauty of your home decor. Be subtle and avoid using patterns that are too distracting in small places. The accentuation of your home's minimalism should include print patterns.

You can match your throw pillows with curtains by choosing a specific pattern. For minimalist decor, you can't go wrong if you choose a simple pattern for your carpet. These patterns add color and texture to minimalism while breaking up the monotony of neutrals and pastels.

It is important to stress that minimalism does not mean that you should sacrifice elegance and beauty. It can even enhance the beauty and elegance of your home's carefully designed objects. If you have too many items in your home, it can create visual distractions and a poor aesthetic. You can make your home beautiful by adopting minimalism.

Chapter 11: Decluttering Mind

We often don't realise that mental clutter is as problematic in our lives, as physical clutter. Mental clutter has taken control of our lives so much that we can no longer think about it. Our mind is always doing something. Your brain begins to get busy the moment you open your eyes in morning. Your brain is either getting ready or brushing your teeth. The one thing missing is the willingness. There is no need, it is just following instructions. These instructions are nothing more than following up with the things of yesterday, commitments, duties, and the like.

We have lost our ability to live our lives as thoughtful, free human beings. Although we are constantly busy making decisions about our lives, most of those decisions are made for us by others.

There is constant pressure on people to save their jobs. The thrill of doing a job well is less than the fear of losing it. While the pay is lower and the experience is smaller, the willingness is high to perform when a person begins a new job. That willingness soon fades because of the pressure to keep the lifestyle and earn more. You stop working on yourself and begin to save the job.

We carry on the company and opinions of people we detest, simply because it's important. It fills up our minds with clutter. We often feel overwhelmed by decision fatigue. We continue to misunderstand. We can't help but plan and plot in our minds, as we are always caught between a devilish and deep blue sea.

These are not without consequences. The mind and body must co-operate. Mental exhaustion can cause serious health problems. It has a profound effect on our behavior. We can't ignore the ones we don't want to. Our relationships start getting strained. Our family lives get affected. Emotional turmoil can cause insecurities, pain, and people look for solace in shopping. People are often compelled to give their time, attention, and compassion to make things right.

Decluttering the mind is an essential part in becoming a minimalist. It can help you organize your mind and determine your priorities. You and your partner both need the same thing most of the time. It can sometimes be difficult to get along. It isn't a lack or coordination. It is the lack or clutter in your environment that causes it.

Once you get your mind sorted and your priorities in place, it will be much easier to connect with and understand your loved ones.

The key is to release the chains and find your true self. To discover what your true desires are, you'll have to do some deep self-introspection. It's important to see the futility of items that don't bring value to your daily life and eliminate them as soon possible. By clearing your mind, you can help your family become a minimalist.

Decluttering

Decluttering means getting rid and donating things, thoughts, people, and other items that don't contribute any real value. Everything you have around must be valuable, and that is why it is so important.

Decluttering Your Home

Decluttering your house will make it easier to manage the Homefront. Decluttering your home will help you feel more relaxed. The feeling of being free from the clutter and things that are not necessary or need maintenance is amazing. This book will walk you through every step of decluttering your home. It is important to remember that every item in your home must be valued.

Your home shouldn't be intimidating, but it shouldn't be a treasure trove that you need to search for items. Everything should be accessible easily and placed in a designated area.

Clear surfaces should be your policy. Clear all flat surfaces including your floors, tabletops, countertops, cabinets, dressers and benches. There are some decorative items you can have, but nothing too large. It is best to remove all unnecessary things from your walls. Keep only those paintings and ornaments that you really value. Don't leave things on your walls just to look good. Be aware that it is difficult to let go of unwanted items at first.

Furniture is essential for a comfortable life. We seldom think about how many pieces of furniture we really need. We tend to buy furniture that we love and then we do not have the mentality to throw away the ones that aren't. Furniture is moved from one room to another. It doesn't serve any purpose and just adds clutter to your home and makes it more difficult to maintain. Determine how much furniture is necessary for your daily life and keep only those pieces. You don't need to keep items in your house if you aren't disturbed by them. This is a bad habit to develop, so it can be difficult to break the cycle.

Then, use the same process to identify your kitchen and bedrooms. You may find your biggest challenge in the wardrobes.

Decluttering is a great way to get control of your home, and your entire life. It is harder to stay in control of your home and life if it becomes more cluttered.

Decluttering Your Head

Decluttering your mind is also important. Mental clutter is the cause of our constant struggle and inability feel the happiness around. Mental clutter causes our minds to become so overloaded with thoughts, that they don't recognize the happiness around.

If your mind is constantly occupied by the chiding your boss is about to give, you can't taste even the best gourmet meal. If you are always late for work, it will make it difficult to enjoy the beauty around you.

It is not just the world that is unhappy but you, the person who has lost your reasons to feel happy. The world remains as beautiful as ever. Rivers still run wild, seas still roaring and mountains still high. The sky is still very bright. We still get soaked by the rain and the morning light still brings out the beauty of the dewdrops.

You can't only see beauty in things. We can't see beauty if we are too focused on our thoughts. We miss the silent pleas made by our loved ones. We neglect to listen to the feelings and concerns of our partners. We suppress our children's cries. Despite all that, we still look outside for love and admiration.

It is impossible to find happiness in life if you don't manage your affairs.

Mental stress is caused by people who are obligated to carry responsibilities they do not want to. This leads to them becoming unhappy and prone to resentful behavior. Give yourself some breathing space. Give yourself some breathing.

It is important to get away from anything that is causing you pain and agony. If you are not enjoying your job, find another one that can bring you happiness. Make it a priority to find time to do things you love. If you find the company and company of only a few people uncomfortable, leave. Avoid lingering.

It is crucial to unclutter your thoughts and reflect on what would bring happiness. An unhappy person spreads more unhappiness.

How to Start

Living a minimalistic lifestyle for your family can seem difficult. It can be difficult to bring the entire family aboard, especially if they don't think the same at first. It's possible, but not impossible. This book will help to explain how you can inspire your family to adopt a minimalist outlook and instill that mindset. It will also provide you with the necessary guidelines for your success.

Keep in mind that this is a brand new path and there may be some bumps along the way. This is normal and will help you lead a more balanced lifestyle. You will find joy and freedom after you have adapted to the lifestyle.

The most important thing is to be reasonable and fair with yourself and family members. Don't force others or hurry the process. It will be something your entire family must enjoy. This might take some time. If you want to live a life of peace, harmony, bliss, and joy, then follow the path that is minimalism.

Chapter 12: Decluttering Guest Rooms & Bedrooms The Minimalist Method

Decluttering your bedroom and guest room are two of the best things you can do to ensure your home is clean. Your bedroom is perhaps the one area of your home that guests should never be allowed in. This is why it's the first place you need to clean out and tidy up in your home. It is your bedroom that you must declutter first. Living minimalistically is possible by removing clutter from your bedroom.

The most common phrase you'll find when looking through content regarding sleeping problems is "peaceful surrounding." A tidy and clean bedroom will help you to get adequate and quality sleep.

Reasons why your bedroom is cluttered

I mentioned before that the bedroom, which is often overlooked by visitors and people in general, is the most important room in our homes. This makes it easier to declutter "public" spaces and forget about bedrooms. It's easy to move clutter from one room to another, particularly if you don't know what you should do with it. If you conceal clutter in your bedroom, it is easy to close the door. Later, even if you want to get rid of the stuff, you will forget.

This makes it worse as clutter attracts more clutter. Over time, everything you've left behind in your bedroom will end up in piles. A minimalist lifestyle requires that you avoid collecting things you don't really use in your home. Your home will be simpler if you know how to clear out clutter in your bedroom.

Declutter Your Bedroom.

What's the point of clearing clutter in your home? Are you really able to see a positive impact on your wellbeing? We previously discussed the benefits and principles that come with living a minimalistic lifestyle.

Your bedroom should be free of clutter so you can rest peacefully after a hard day. Decluttering your bedroom allows you to unwind and recharge after a stressful day.

A bedroom that is cluttered with stuff can be a very stressful place. The clutter and possessions in your bedroom serve as reminders of what you have to do.

Minimalist Ways to Declutter Your Bedroom & Guests Room

Did you also know that clutter in the bedroom can reduce your energy levels? If you truly want to clear your bedroom of clutter, you need to decide not to allow junk from other parts of your home to be kept in it. You must have a place in your bedroom to put every item. A piece of furniture that does more than one task is usually a good idea.

Set a clear vision in your space

Now, let's begin! The vision you have for your bedroom should be clear. You want it to look good, feel right and work well. To begin decluttering your bedroom, you need to first have a clear idea and vision. Only keep those things that will support your vision of a minimalist lifestyle and home.

Identify your room's purpose!

What does your bedroom symbolize to you? Is it a sanctuary from the chaos and stress of life? It's important that you define it. This will help you determine how you want to use it.

If your bedroom is a place where you sleep, your decluttering needs should be considered. There will not be much furniture beyond a bed and a dressing table. You can make your home as functional or beautiful as you like.

The picture below shows a minimalist bedroom

Now that you have a picture of what your bedroom should look like, let's take a look at what is in there. Do you love all of the things that are stacked in your bedroom, or is it a burden? What purpose are they serving? Are you actually using them for their intended uses? It doesn't mean that you have to give up on things that add no value to your daily life. Every item in your bedroom should support your vision.

Perhaps you have an armchair in a bedroom. But are you using it as a chair to sit in when you wake up in the morning? Or is it something you use to hang your clothes, as well as those you plan on washing. You can keep your armchair in your bedroom, provided you're not using it as a clutter collector. This is also true for other things that don't serve their intended purpose. You can remove them.

A minimalist bedroom has modern furniture, solid colours, and sleek interiors. If you're naturally neat and tidy, you might find it easy to put away your shoes or clothes. If you aren't, it can be difficult keeping your bedroom clear of clutter. If you are looking to live in a clutter-free bedroom, it is important that you adopt a minimalist design.

This should reflect in your furniture choices. If you have the chance, it would be a great idea to clean out your bedroom completely and then start again. Create a list that includes everything you need for your bedroom. Make sure you evaluate them before buying. Do these items really serve a purpose?

If you aren't certain whether or not you need it, you can take any item off the list. If you find that the bathroom mirror is more convenient for your needs, it might be worth removing the dressing room table from the list. If you don't mind leaving books on your floor, you may have to add a table to the bedside.

Clean the room

You can label the boxes using the box method. One box is needed for each category.

Trash

Donate

Keep

If you wish to alter the furniture, it can be removed. You will notice that your room looks messy at first. However, things get better over time. It is important to organize all boxes, including your donation box, so that you can bring out items from your room and then place them where they belong. You've already described the idea of a minimalist space, so let that guide you in placing each item in different boxes. You'll soon discover how many things you really don't need in your bedroom.

Get in touch with your needs

Now that you have taken inventory of everything in your room, think about where you would like it to be. You can now bring in your things and change what you don't want, like furniture.

Furniture

You might be surprised at how much you like the design of the existing furniture. Is it compatible with your minimalist style? The floor should be as wide as possible. This can be achieved by adding a few items to your space. The illusion of less clutter and more space is created when shelves are suspended from the walls rather than on the floors. Choose furniture that is pleasing to your eye and doesn't stand out. It should blend into the background.

Electronics in your bedroom

Even if you keep your room tidy, it is likely that there are electrical cables. Because we often use our phones, tablets and laptops in our bedrooms, it is easy to forget about the chargers or cables that are also lying around on the floor. These devices are often in constant use so it can be hard to put them away. Alternative options include integrating them into your bedroom.

You could, for example, run cables along baseboards. After that, apply the same colour of paint to the baseboards to blend them in. To make it easier to clean up the chargers when you're done, keep the socket accessible. One socket should be designated for charging, to stop cables from getting lost in the corners.

Your storage

Your goal is to organize your space but you still want it fully functional - such as a bedroom. Your bedroom should have a minimal look. Make sure everything is in an easily accessible place. If you use your bedside table to store your tablet, books and laptops, or their cables, you'll need a closet.

If you don't need an extra chair, it is worth considering incorporating storage into the window seat. This will allow you to have easy access storage. Dressers large enough to accommodate hairdressers, straighteners and other items are required unless they are kept in the bathroom.

Clear away clutter

It is important to eliminate clutter from the surfaces of your home. It is easy for items to accumulate on these flat surfaces. Get rid of all the clutter you can see, including shelves, dressers, floor, and nightstands.

Take it one step at a while and take out everything you don't use or love. You can keep everything you want to get rid of where it belongs. Remember that clutter is always created by the things that have no home. So, if you don't need them, find a home for them. This would stop them from cluttering up your flat surfaces.

Decor

It is also important to assess your room decor items. These include decorative pillows and wall hangings, bedding, decorative objects, window treatments, and decorative objects. A simple way to make your bedroom appear cleaner and more tranquil is to get rid of all unnecessary decor. Do not rush to replace any decor items that aren't necessary or you love. It's a good idea to try living without them for some time and see if you really miss them.

Clothes

Clothes are one of the most common sources of clutter and can often be a challenge when it comes to decluttering bedrooms. Don't let clothes get in the way of your enjoyment. You know what works for you. Do you find it overwhelming to organize all your clothes or do you prefer to work on one drawer at the time? Decide which one is the best and follow it. Spend some time sorting through each drawer, and make sure you only keep the things you really need.

How to Make Your Bedroom Clean After Decluttering

Now that you know the best ways to declutter your bedroom it is time to figure out how to keep it clean. To keep your bedroom clutter free, you must adopt a minimalist approach to living.

Everything should have its place. As we have discussed, clutter is often caused by stuff that doesn't have a home. If they don't have any place to keep them, they end-up being clutter on flat surfaces like floors and tables. You will be able to easily locate each item and put them away. Find the most clutter-prone items in your bedroom, and make a space for them. To make your bedroom clutter-free, you might have a small storage container to hold keys, jewelry, wallets, or change. Your bedroom should not be a place to store random items from other rooms, especially if you don't know what they belong to. Protect your space that you have just decluttered. Make it a tranquil place.

Make your bed every morning. It's easy to instantly transform the way your bedroom feels and looks. A tidy bed will make your bedroom feel more spacious, calmer, and easier to use. It inspires you not only to tidy up your bed but also the rest.

Daily bedroom reset: Another great habit you can develop to keep your bedroom clean is to do a daily bedroom reset. This is when you clean up the room and put away all of your clutter. It allows you to manage clutter before it becomes overwhelming. Try to take a minute each day to clean up your laundry and tidy up the surfaces. This will make it easy to maintain a tidy bedroom.

Place your clothes in order: A pile of clothes scattered around your bedroom will make it appear cluttered and chaotic. A laundry basket is a great place to keep your dirty clothes. It is important to have space for clothes that you will re-wear to avoid stacking them up. You can store them on a closet shelf, or somewhere else in your room. It's important to have a designated place for your clothes in order to prevent them from becoming "homeless." Decluttering your bedroom makes it simple to put your clean clothes away.

Organizing your Bedroom

You shouldn't organise your room until you have cleared out all clutter. After you've decluttered your bedroom, you must organize the items that you keep in a fashion that makes sense. Now that your bedroom is clear of clutter, it's much easier to organize it. What is the best organizing system for you? A minimalist's goal is to minimize how many things you have stored.

Bedroom Decorating

After you've decluttered your bedroom, and created new habits, it's time to transform your space into a space you love coming to every day. The next step is to transform your bedroom into your private oasis. This can include changing your bedding, painting the walls in a favorite color, and other tasks.

Do not rush decorating your bedroom. Take your time and be thoughtful. Add decorative elements slowly and with care to your bedroom, taking into consideration the budget and time constraints. Make sure that the decorative items you add are compatible with a minimalist bedroom and your original vision of your bedroom. You have to love your bedroom as much as the items inside it. Keep your bedroom clutter-free and less expensive. It doesn't necessarily mean you should spend a lot on furniture. Get the things you truly love and value in your room. Decorating isn't about cluttering your space.

Chapter 13: Think Small, Live Big

Minimalism can often be associated with bland colors and empty spaces. A minimalist image is one that features large homes with lots of open space, straight lines, glass, or neutral colors. But this is only one way to achieve minimalism. You can alter the dimensions of any space. Minimal design demands that you minimize the clutter in your home. You have to be willing to live small and think big. Your ability to think small while living large requires that you find creative ways in which to bring big-scale design ideas to your space. It's all about making use of your space to create a space that is comfortable and makes you feel fulfilled. Your home should be somewhere you feel comfortable spending your time. You must first think about the kind of space that you want. Clear intentions will help you design your space with purpose. It's possible for a small area to be your dream space. Your key to success is to shift your perspective and explore different uses for your small space.

You can implement large-scale designs in your space by following this principle. Consider why you are attracted to a space, design, concept, or idea. Do you love the effects, colors, patterns, combinations, and shapes? The best way to make your space more appealing is to find out what you like about the design. Feeling inspired by a space, design, idea, or other aspect of it can help you to feel. These feelings can be imitated in your space.

Once you've determined which elements of the design you want, you can begin work on your floorplan. Your floorplan is the way you plan to divide your space. You will be shown the original layout of a space if it has been occupied by a previous owner. The rooms are labeled according their intended use, but you don't have to follow these guidelines. If you don't need a spare room, transform the space into one that suits your requirements. Your space should be purposeful. This is the best way for you to think big in small spaces. Plan how you'd like to use the space. This will help you optimize your space. It is possible to create spaces that can serve multiple purposes by looking at the different areas within your home. Then, sketch your space on paper. You will label the different areas. Alternate the areas until it works for you. This is an important step in any space. You can show how you intend on using it. Once you have created a plan and are able to visualize the spaces you desire in your home, it's time for you to start implementing your design.

Design Tips

With your inspirations as a guide, you can create design tips to maximize the space and achieve your desired effect. It is possible to create the illusion of a bigger space by thinking big. Even though your space may be small, it does not mean your design decisions should be. Your space should feel bigger by adding more light. Light, both natural and artificial, can open up spaces and create a welcoming space. White walls can help achieve the same effect. White walls will give off a more spacious feeling and give the illusion that your space is bigger. The same effect can be achieved by solid-colored walls. Use bright paint colors and plenty of light to make your space feel bigger. The space will also grow if you make bold decisions.

The vertical space is a great way to maximize your space. Your vertical space will help you add height to your home regardless of how high the walls are. You can emphasize vertical space by using stripes, wall hanging and higher rails. Hanging decorative items, such as shelves, will draw your attention to the ceiling when you enter your house. It creates the illusion you have higher ceilings. Use a themed wallpaper to create a bold statement in the home. A feature wall adds visual interest to a room. This wall is an opportunity to be creative and fun in your home. I suggest muted-colored stripes so as to not overwhelm the space or create an area that is difficult for your eyes.

Your furniture selection can have a significant impact on how your space looks. For smaller spaces, you might want to consider buying smaller versions of quality furniture. A smaller version of your dream furniture can be reproduced at a lower cost and will provide you with durable pieces. Online shopping is a great way to find affordable custom furniture or talk to local dealers about customizing an existing item. You can save money by reducing the size of your item. The same design can be adapted to a two-seater loveseat, instead of a large four-seater couches that take up space in your home. You can choose the colors and patterns you want, as well as the textures, that you want in your space. You have the chance to choose durable, expensive fabrics for a fraction off the cost due to the dimensions of your piece. Selling your existing furniture can help you save money and cover the cost associated with downsizing. Be aware of this when you move into a smaller space. Large furniture shouldn't take over the space. Any furniture piece can be customized to meet your specific needs. You should make your couch a focal point in your home. It is a key piece in any space that guides your design decisions.

Be mindful of how furniture is used in your home. Multipurpose furniture can be a way to reduce furniture clutter. Multipurpose furniture is furniture that is designed to be used for multiple activities. Hidden storage can be found in a stool meant for seating. A couch that doubles up as a second bed can save you space and allow you to use the same room for both purposes. There are many ways that you can incorporate this furniture into your space. Your space should feel welcoming and open. This can be achieved by selecting minimal furniture. Multipurpose furniture can maximize your space's potential by serving multiple functions. You can bring life and vitality to your space by including plants. There are many indoor plant options that you can use to brighten up your space. Different plants require different amounts of maintenance. If you don't enjoy caring for plants, or are a committed plant killer, you may want to try a plant that needs little to no maintenance, like a Cactus. Plants give us purpose and responsibility. It is satisfying to see their growth and transformation throughout the seasons.

You have two options to design your home. Either you break it up with dividers (or go for an open-plan approach). Both options have advantages and disadvantages, depending upon what kind of space is being used. You can make your space more private and have specific areas created. You can create a private space in your bedroom by adding dividers to an open space. This helps you create privacy when guests visit your home. You can find dividers that match your space, or customize premade wooden ones with paint and templates. These dividers don't have to be boring. This is vital because a divider is a constant divider in your space. You can use a different design on each side of your room divider to allow you to switch between them (Medeiros (2013)).

Open-plan layouts, in contrast, allow for continuous flow and give the illusion of more space. You won't feel restricted by walls that enclose the space. A home with an open layout will only require one design. A neutral palette combined with small pops are a great way to decorate your home. You can alter the decorative pieces in the home to create different pops of color. Because of its freedom, an open plan can be very effective in minimalist design. To reduce the size of your belongings, you can downsize. Living in a smaller area allows you to be more flexible and helps you understand your priorities. A tiny home is a space that you can use to live a minimalistic life. Tiny homes can help you think big while living in a small space.

Because of the popularity of minimalism as well as social media, tiny houses have gained in popularity. Tiny homes allow people to save money while still living in their dreams. Tiny homes can be a good option if you are looking for off-grid, or remote living. But, it is possible to live in an apartment in a large city or in the suburbs. Tiny homes are a great way to have freedom and mobility. You have options. You can park your mobile house in designated areas. Tiny homes are a good way to make small changes in your life and practice minimalism. They are more environmentally friendly and will reduce your carbon footprint. You have two options. One, you can purchase pre-built tiny homes. Two, you can build your own. Many minimalists prefer self-builds. This saves money and allows them to customize their space. You should consider the future when planning your self-build. Tiny homes show you how to live with less and less space. By requiring you to use your space effectively, tiny homes can increase your creativity. If you are looking to make a significant change in your life and home, you might want to consider investing. Although it may seem overwhelming at first, the initial cost is less than traditional homes.

Minimalism should be about quality and not quantity. Instead of clogging up your space, surround yourself only with what you really need. Spend time decorating your home and choosing design aesthetics you love. Slowly decorating your home will allow you to take time to ensure your space is perfect. You will also save money by not waiting for sales at retailers and shopping from thrift shops and markets. Be patient and make sure that you are satisfied with the items in each space. To think big in small spaces, you need to have an open mind. Let your creativity shine through your space. Your home should reflect the personality and interests of you.

Chapter 14: Cultivating Digital Minimalism Behaviors

Habits are created by the mind. To understand how habits affect our mind, we must first understand what they are.

Additionally, it is necessary to understand the nature of habits and how they were formed.

Habit Formation and Nature

Habits are repetitive patterns of behavior that result from repetitive words, actions, or thoughts.

Habit formation is done by the habit loop. This habit loop contains trigger, routine and reward.

A trigger is triggered when a certain event occurs. A cue simply refers to a recollected event that triggers an automatic trigger.

It is the action that becomes a habit when a certain action happens based upon a trigger. A routine is simply repetitive actions that follow a specific pattern. This repetition will guide your behavior. You should remember that routines represent work. A routine is work done by following a pattern.

The reward must motivate people to do the routine. The reward is a mechanism to pay for the routine effort. This motivates or incentives the continuation of a routine. If there is no reward, there are no incentives or motivations for continuing the routine.

The Nature of a HabitCue

A habit cue describes a mental image associated to a positive past experience.

Digital habit cues can be found here:

* Push-up notification reminding that you have a new post in social media.

* A PC reminder reminding you of the start to the holiday season

* A smartphone flashlight indicating that you have received an SMS.

The Nature of a Trigger

Cue is often used interchangeably with trigger in habit formation. However, they do not have to be synonymous.

A trigger can be described as a mental button that's activated when a cue is received. A cue could be defined as a preliminary occurrence that triggers an alert and then routes the response to it. That response can be rewarded with a reward.

Digital Triggers - Examples

* A greetings message pops up whenever you visit any site or click a button

* A pop-up fill-in that appears when you close a specific webpage.

Routine is part of the human condition

A routine refers to a mental program that automates repetitive sequences of actions and events. A routine is a mental programme that guides a specific behavior.

These routines can include: waking up at an agreed time, breakfast routing, reading, flossing, brushing teeth, washing your face, dressing for the day, packing lunches, eating at specific times, attending classes at particular hours, etc.

Here are some of the common digital routines

* Read email before going to bed

* Instantly after eating breakfast, visit news websites

* The evening social

Positive effects of a constructive routine

A positive routine has an impact on your health and well-being. It will help you be better in every aspect of your life: relationships, education, career, wealth and other areas.

Constructive Digital Routines

You can batch digital tasks so that they are completed at a set time. This could be, for example, digital mailing, social-media posting, or telephone calls that are batched so you can complete them in the afternoon before your workday ends.

A few of the Positive Effects Common to a Constructive Practice

* More efficient performance in repetitive tasks

* Greater efficiency, effectiveness

* Higher levels accuracy

* Greater productivity

* Standardization of control mechanism: measurement, evaluation, and remedial measures.

Negative effects of a destructive routine

A destructive routine is one that adversely impacts your wellbeing. A harmful routine will hinder your growth and development, in vital areas, like your relationships, education career, wealth, health, wealth, and other faculties.

Destructive Digital Routines

* You are too busy to check social media after you wake up and end up late at work or poorly prepared for your day.

* Playing videogames right before falling asleep so that you have a delayed sleep.

The following are the negative effects of a harmful digital routine:

* Digital addiction

* Declined productivity

* Insomnia (due a late-night, digital addiction)

The Reward's Nature

It's obvious that routines can be considered work. Every task comes with a reward. The appreciation of the reward helps to reinforce and feed the habit loop.

A monetary payment can come in the form or a salary, wage, commission or royalty. An alternative reward is a non-monetary one.

Psychological (e.g.. motivation and induction), actualization, fulfillment, etc.),

Emotional (e.g., love, affection, friendship, mentorship, etc.),

Spiritual (e.g., peace, serenity, joy, happiness, etc.),

Mental (e.g., exam grades, certificates, diplomas, degrees, etc.),

Physical (e.g.: a hug or kiss, sexual intercourse etc.),

A combination of both non-monetary and monetary forms.

Digital Reward Examples

* A friend shared a humorous emoji for a nice comment on digital media.

* An honor (e.g. Spider Solitaire Fireworks) for winning a digital app

* Reward points if you perform well

Digital Minimalism Tips You Should Adopt

* Keep your apps minimal and the most important.

* Delete data you no longer need

* Keep your digital trash emptied often

* Save data that isn't important and is not used often in cloud storage so your smartphone load is minimal

* Define a time when you will be able to read emails and respond to them. This will ensure that you do not allow your inbox to overflow.

* Turn off your electronic devices when you go to bed

* You should keep digital gadgets out of your bedroom. Even the alarm-clock should be out of your bedroom

* Keep your eyes off of social media networks during study/work hours. After work/study, do that at night.

* Reduce your online presence to less then an hour per session, only a few times per week

* Only one social media account will be closed.

* Choose one email and close the rest

* Unsubscribe from unrelated social media, news or email feeds

* Don't allow unnecessary push notifications

* Do away with smartphones Instead, you can use your normal phone for calling and SMS. Use your desktop computer instead, if you must read email or surf the internet.

* Don't take your smartphone with you wherever you go.

Bad Digital Habits you Need to Get Rid of

Eliminating the Bad Habits

Just like bad habits can be created, bad habits can also be killed. These are the ways that you can eliminate bad habits.

1. Get stronger in your willpower

2. Boost your self-awareness

3. Gather emotional support

4. Engage in sublimation

5. You can substitute

6. Establish and implement habit stacks

Strengthen Your Willpower

Will is closely related to desire. If you don't want it very much, your willpower to succeed is likely weak.

Dependent on what we desire, our desire can be either positive or negative. To achieve your full potential, you must have good desires. They will give you the fuel you need to push forward.

Get more self-awareness

Self-awareness refers the ability to be aware of one's personality, feelings and motivations. To be self aware is to know and understand yourself. If you discover who and what you are, then you can establish your purpose and use your willpower in pursuing it.

Gather Emotional support

Bad habits die hard. Not telling your loved ones and trusted friends about them can be detrimental. It's important to have the support of your family members and close friends when you are trying to break bad habits. They will provide support, advice, and understanding to help you overcome your challenges. They may even offer a reward for you success. This makes it harder to stop committing bad behavior.

Participate in Sublimation

Sublimation is a way to replace a primitive urge for a more creative one. You can play tennis or the piano if you feel a sexual craving that will push you to online pornographic websites. While you may not have been able to satisfy your primal desire for sex (although you did suppress it), you are able to replace it with a more creative urge to play the piano. Sublimation means replacing one urge for another without offering an alternative.

Substitution

Substitution is when you find a better alternative to satisfy the same urge. As an example, if social media addiction is a problem, you might be able to overcome it by taking part in social events at your local community rather than going online. This will fulfill your desire to socialize by substituting virtual for actual. This is called substitution. It doesn't suppress your desire to socialize but provides a better solution.

Create Habit Stacks

You can quickly get rid of bad habits with habit stacking.

Chapter 15: How To Organize Your Home Office

Working from home is something that more people are accepting and understanding in our modern world. It can be wonderful to work remotely but there are downsides. Some of the disadvantages include the ease at which work and your family can mix without making clear distinctions. Also, the stress of finding the right workspace in the home.

To be a successful home-based entrepreneur, you will need more than just your business savvy and grit. It is essential that you understand how to effectively manage your time to get the best results from working remotely. You need to think about where your workspace will be placed in your home. Let's talk about the various options available to you and how you can create a more organized space that helps you be more productive.

It's time to get started

First, you have to identify what clutter has been accumulated and take out all items that are cluttering that space. It could be the bookshelves or the drawer underneath your desk. No matter what the clutter is, it's important to get rid of everything that may be in these spaces. In order to prevent accidental blending, you need to clearly define the boundaries between the two spaces.

The Paper Clutter

The main cause of office clutter is paper. Paper, paper. Even with the current "digitalization" of the business environment, it's still difficult to live without them. You can avoid them by learning how to handle them. There are always lots of them just waiting to be addressed. The largest pile should be chosen and you can start your work.

Each receipt, flyer or document will have to be read. You'll need to go through each receipt, document, flyer and script you find. Not only will you find lots of fascinating information, but you'll also be reminded of your past. This is not a time to go back and look at vacation photos or read through magazine articles. You have to get it done as fast as possible. If the paper isn't essential, it's not life or death. There's no reason to save it for later. You may never need it again if the year is over.

Create a classification system for documents that you may need. The main categories of paper in your office can be classified into the following: bank statements and receipts, investments records, financial statements, insurance information, etc. It all depends on how many documents you use in your office. This classification makes it easier for you to find the documents you need, rather than having a messy pile of papers that frustrates.

The Office Desk

The office desk functions as a workspace. As such, it must have sufficient space to allow you to feel comfortable.

The first thing to remember is that only the essentials you use every day should be kept in your office. This will include your computer, a notebook, and a pencil. The rest should be stored in a drawer until they are needed. The ideal decluttered desk space allows you to relax on your bench and extend your arm as far on the workspace as possible, without any hindrance. Some of your personal belongings can be placed on the table, including family photos. However, you must know where to draw the line to ensure that the workspace doesn't get cluttered.

Once you have created these categories, you can now determine how many drawers will be required to file them properly. Depending upon their size and contents, you could place several folders in one drawer. The drawer that contains a particular type of paper should be the closest to you. You should place folders that are more frequently used in the drawer closest to your face.

The Paper Bills

Because it is so important, you should note when your bills are due. The timing of your payments will vary between people, so you should be specific about the date you are going to pay them.

Subscribe to an automatic payment option if your bill forgetting is a problem. This will let you pay your bills in a way that you are not aware of. Another way is to give the bill settlement to a family member that's organized and competent with finances.

It's best to have a consistent system in place to handle all the paperwork that comes in. There may not have been a formal system for dealing with paperwork. This is why you need to set one up now. It's very easy to do and I will provide you with helpful guidelines. These tips are helpful:

You should first place papers in the right category. This should be an easy task you can do at least once each day. The important thing is to make sure that every paper that comes in each day is placed in a new place before the day ends. You won't be able handle all the papers in one sitting, but it is a good start to make the job easier and declutter the area for any incoming paper.

Each category or paper classification comes with a specific action. All bills must be paid. Mails must be answered quickly. Questions should be answered promptly and returned. All of these are actions that are related to these papers. This will help you to know your goals before you begin to work on the papers.

Consider the possibility that you are responsible for many papers in your work space. A larger area should be allocated to filing these papers. The amount you use of paper per day will be the major factor in determining the right space to allocate for it.

How to handle digital clutter within your work space

The digital realm of the internet is continually evolving. Every day, there are new software, apps, and computer programs that make life easier. The possibilities of studying digital clutter are many. Although one method might be effective for you today it could soon become obsolete after three months. This is why you should learn to move with time.

This section will briefly explore how we can keep our digital lives in check and manage digital clutter.

The computer system is where most of the stuff that we digitally live, so organizing it will be our primary focus. These tips will help you get there.

It is essential that your files are stored in a central location. This means that your digital files need to be organized so that any stranger can easily locate your files. Some people find it difficult to find digital files in the computer system. It's not difficult to see how dangerous this can be. By using a centralized and well-organized system, it is easy to locate the needed file in a short scan.

After creating a centralized system, you will need to develop a method for managing your files. You should classify your files according to the contents. It is easier to find them this manner.

To increase your computer's storage space, you can upload files to cloud storage. Cloud Me and Microsoft One Drive are some of the online storage options that you have, as well as Dropbox. The best thing to do is to research them all and select the one that you like.

Digital Clutter also covers the time we spend online using social media platforms. How do manage your online time? Do you spend hours scrolling through Instagram meme pages and watching Instagram skits? It's okay to have some fun. But you will eventually become overwhelmed and lose sight the most important things. This is the opposite of minimalism. These two tools will allow you to find the most important items in your life. It is important to have a policy that allows you to return to productive mode after having had fun.

Emails must be dealt with as quickly as possible. They shouldn't pile up and overwhelm you. It is nearly impossible to eliminate all emails from your inbox daily. But you should make an effort to remove one per day. At most, you can manage and respond to 20 email per day. This allows you to reduce the work load. Also, set aside a certain time every day to answer emails. You should not do this out of the blue.

Reduce the number of items on your desktop so that only the most critical folders or files can be found. It's not smart to clutter up your desktop with files or folders. By grouping like content into one main directory, you can make it much easier.

Electronics and Cables

Electronics are going to be around for a long time. You should know how to protect your workspace from them. A new electronic gadget will require extra care. If you are willing to spend a little more and get the same results, why not just buy the equipment? Photocopying is an example. It takes up a lot in your office so it is worth the investment. You can also borrow one from a neighbor or use theirs quickly.

Chapter 16: Minimalism And Fashion

The phrase "minimalist fashion" is likely to bring up only a handful. Perhaps you picture thin, ungainly pieces of clothing that look like nothing.

Maybe it is associated with a general mood. It might excite you, as getting dressed in a morning will be much more easy. Or it may make your skin shiver.

Although they are all pieces of a larger piece, they do not give a complete picture about minimalist fashion.

A minimalist fashion style includes a light, neutral-filled outfit. This is the minimalist fashion aesthetic. The white walls of a house will show a hint of colour, which is similar to minimalist furniture styles. You can have hundreds of clothes in your closet and still have minimalistic styling.

The minimalistic approach to fashion is as individual as the minimalistic look. It's not all about what color you use or how many clothes you have, but about your attitude and the idea behind the clothes.

Fashion is best when you are mindful of your style and not trying to buy the most. You want to have a wardrobe with quality pieces that you love, and that will last many years.

The goal is to not reduce your wardrobe below ten. The goal isn't to have just black, grey and gold sun specks. It is not to make you hate your clothes. In reality, it's quite the opposite.

Did you realize that the average person only wears 20% of their wardrobe every day? This means that about 80% of the clothes we feel comfortable living without end up hanging in our closets. While we reach for the exact same dress or sweater every day, it is likely that only 20% of the items we love are actually worn regularly.

If you've ever looked in your closet, and decided that there was nothing you could wear, this is most likely not the case. This could be a sign that you are suffering from decision fatigue. The paradox of choice is a term that states that the more options, the harder it is to make the right decision.

But what if it doesn't happen to your future? What if every day you opened your closet and found the only items you love? So that everything you wear makes you feel beautiful, confident, and unquestionably yourself? So, what options are there?

My recommendation? Get rid of everything in your closet.

Because you want that amazing feeling of being able look through your closet without judging what you like.

There are many things that could tempt you to consider the question: "How did we get here?"

Chances are, that looking through your closet can be overwhelming. However decluttering it is the first step to achieving your ideal wardrobe.

THE FOUR PILES

Everything is removed from your wardrobe and chests of drawers, and laid on your bed. This will allow you to get to sleep and organize your belongings before you wake up.

There are four piles which follow the "love", "maybe", "no" and "cyclical," piles after you have taken everything out of one giant pile.

The heap of "love"

There are the items you feel a deep love for. These items are easy to spot because they would be worn every day.

A heap of "no Thanks"

If you see something in "nope", you know you won't wear it again. These garments are rarely taken out.

The "possible" List.

Things become confused in the "maybe" pile. These are those things that, for reasons unknown to you, are not in the "love", "nope" or "nope basket. It is possible that they are no longer fitting as well as they once did. It may not fit well, as the zipper is broken, seams are torn, and the straps need to adjusted. It could be that you once loved them, but now don't, or it may bring back fond childhood memories. It doesn't even matter what kind of clothes it is, it will not fit into the "nope", and "love", piles.

Pile of "repeated", items

Depending on where it is located, you might or may not need the "cyclical". It is beneficial for the seasons. It's for you if the seasons change regularly and you require specific pieces of clothing for each. When it is time for de-cluttering, the "cyclical" pile is determined only by the seasons.

If you are clearing out clutter in the spring or summer, this pile will have boots, pullovers and thick coats.

If you are clearing out clutter in the fall and mid-winter months, such items as trunks, tank tops and flip-flops should go in the pile. You can test them now instead of waiting to see if you will wear them in the next three to six month.

Return every item to the "loved" pile and place it back in its original place in your closet. Then, put your "cyclical", or pile of items, in a box. This will allow you to keep it for future reference. Analytical minimalism is now possible.

Start with your "love," and "no", piles that are currently hanging in your closet. Then look for design matches.

Your favourite items, and some you don't hesitate getting rid of, may have similarities in colour, line, fabric or other aspects. You can take notes with your phone or on a notepad while looking for similarities. It's possible that you will need them again in the future.

The "maybe" pile should be the next. You'll be looking for similar designs or similarities this time. While your favourite shirt may be scratchy but you still love it, you might have some shirts similar to it. A couple of outfits will stand out if you have shorter straps. Note any thing that gives you inspiration to make your minimalist wardrobe.

Time for Decision

If you are looking to get rid of your "nope", then you need to decide whether to sell, gift, or dispose of it. If they look great but do not suit your personal style, it may be worth selling or donating them. If they are too damaged to be sold or donated, you might think of reusing them. If you don't need any of these, you have two options: throw it away, or donate it at a nearby textile recycling center.

Go through your notes and use your "maybe" pile to review your list. Please note any items that are perfect if tailored. Be sure to keep track if you have clothing that would look better in different fabrics.

If you find your "love" pile lacking in products, consider adding some of your favorites to the "maybe" pile. After that, stockpile all the rest. You should keep the box for a certain period of storage, such as three to six months. If you haven't used or craved any items from the box, it might time to throw it out.

It's now time to breathe after all this is over.

Give yourself time to adjust when you go from Kaleidoscopic to a more minimalistic and intentional approach to slow-fashion. It is best to start now to find the camaraderie with your favourite characters. A reduced wardrobe allows you to be more aware and conscious of the items you love and those you don't.

What defines your style?

Once you have organized your closet, the next step will be to define your personal style.

The contrast between your style & your clothes is likened to the distinction between de-cluttering & ultimate simplicity. Your wardrobe is your fashion gear, while style is how you express yourself through your clothes choices.

It is a given that you will have a wardrobe. But if you don't take the time to create your style, your closet may end up looking just as chaotic as before you started your minimalist journey.

How do you describe your personal style, if any?

Visualize what you are wearing.

Visualizing one's style is a great way to get started. You can pin and save any item that represents you personal style to a virtualboard or a labelled folder on your PC desktop.

There may be full-length gowns, coiffures, cosmetics and ornaments, tabloid shots, or even color palettes.

Identify your wardrobe pattern.

Every so often, it is important that you take stock of what your personal style looks like compared to other styles.

Pay close attention to colours and patterns you are drawn to. It is not uncommon for a certain style to be seen, such as a specific silhouette, styling choice and dress formula. Look at color and patterns along with subtle details such how the item shutters, fabric type or unique elements that make a garment superficial.

You can compare what you did during the Decluttering phase to see how it compares. Begin by determining the style of your current walk-in closet and what you would like to see in the future.

Practicality is key to minimalist fashion.

It's all about experimentation when it comes to minimalist fashion.

Start by looking at the styling tips, accent colours, silhouettes and styling tricks you have saved on your style board. It will encourage you to think outside the box and enable you to envision your reality in action as well.

It may look great on photos but it doesn't necessarily translate into how you feel. Is there something about these shoes that makes it so difficult to maintain daily?

Adopt color palettes.

Experimenting and trying different colors and styles will help to discover the style that suits you best.

It is easier and more cost-effective to mix and match colours. You can keep to a defined colour scheme, which includes primary colours, neutrals, and accent shades. It is not easy to choose the right colour scheme for you. But, in the end you will have a vibrant but versatile wardrobe.

Instead of worrying whether your colors will complement or clash with one another, it is possible to arrange them on distinct objects that can't be mixed. This is a great alternative strategy for those who don't like the idea using just neutrals or a single color palette.

Conclusion

It is crucial that we realize the true utility and value of all possessions in our lives. Otherwise, material possessions can dominate our feelings and overtake our happiness. If we limit our attention to material possessions, then our life is dominated by the material. This view can reduce our ability to see the bigger picture, which can lead us to overlook other aspects of our lives. It is important not to be greedy about the material things of this world. Instead, we should look at the real purpose of our lives and find those most valuable to us. You have the option to sell or donate family possessions. You can get rid of clothes, decorations, and cookware if desired. You may occasionally be able to take away your furniture, tools, books, toys and any other items that are not necessary. It will reflect your lifestyle and allow you to view your life with full strength.

Intentionally choosing to live with minimal will result in great consequences. You can see why minimalism is so popular. Many people strive to live a minimalistic lifestyle for better living.

Being minimalist means living simply. But living simple may not be easy. Living simple can lead to stress reduction and other benefits. The minimalist lifestyle will bring you happiness and plenty of free time. You will not want to go back in time to your chaotic past lifestyle.

However, it is important to embrace challenges in order maintain a simple, stress free lifestyle. A minimalist life and home requires hard work and great determination to succeed. You will need to put in a lot effort to live this lifestyle. In today's society, simple living can be difficult to grasp.

This process is not simple. You need to be open to facing many challenges and difficulties. Every minimalist must confront both their inner and outer resistance during the initial phase. To become a minimalist and to create the minimalist home you must overcome many obstacles. You can learn how to overcome these obstacles if you are starting to be minimalist or you want to become minimalist.

The eradication process is never stopped.

It's not easy to keep a minimalist home. You may be surprised at how many things you have left behind after getting rid of everything that is not essential.

Purging can become an inexorable chore. This is why you should perform the purge after a specified time. This process can be very frustrating for minimalists. This can be frustrating for minimalists. However, if you have the ability to get involved with all of your family members and do it deliberately, it shouldn't be that difficult. It's a process that you have to go through repeatedly in order to get rid your possessions. Clearing one area in your house will make it easier for you to make it a regular routine.

A minimalist house is a wonderful place for many happiness. This home is clean and minimalist, and it encourages a healthy lifestyle of less. The benefits of having lots of space can be a source for mental peace. But it can be hard to keep a minimalist space. While it's true that minimalists face different challenges when arranging their minimalist homes, this is not a surprise. Maintaining a minimalist home means you have to confront many challenges. It is essential to approach these challenges strategically. Otherwise, you might lose the core of your minimalist house. Maintaining your minimalist home is vital if you want to continue living a minimalist lifestyle. We'll discuss smart ways to maintain your minimalist-style home.

You must be very selective about what you allow to your living space. It is important to consider the utility of the product in your daily life. Are you able to add value to your own life or help you achieve your life goals with this product? If you get a yes, then buy it. If it isn't, leave it. If you are an aspiring artist and you love to create craft items, then you may need crafting supplies to help you maintain your artistic life. You can make your home messy if you don't have the time to craft or buy a lot of items at stores that won't be used again. It's the same when your relatives or friends give you gifts that aren't needed for your daily life or home. It is best to ask your friends and relatives to refrain from sending a gift to yourself and your family. They can, however, donate it to any charitable organization or social organization in your area. This can lead to clutter in the home. It is important to think before you act if you don't want your home or lifestyle to become cluttered.

A clutter-free home requires you to be active every day. You shouldn't be lazy about getting rid all the junk in your home.

You'll live a happier life in a minimalist environment. You can take an immediate step to eliminate any useless items from your house. To make your life more stress-free, get rid of all those unnecessary items. However, to achieve this goal, you need to compile a list and create a simple routine to keep your living space clean. This is where you will decide if the products are worth keeping in your home. If you feel that these products aren't necessary, then throw them in the trash or donate them to charity. Your mailbox should be clutter-free. It can be applied to every aspect of your day. It's not necessary to feel guilty about keeping unnecessary items in your room. Your stuff should be removed with a lot of courtesy. Throw away the old products after purchasing any new shampoos or cosmetics.

It doesn't make you rude to someone who is offering something to your needs. We live in a society, and we must have different relations with each other. Some are our family members, some are our friends, some are neighbors. Most of them are kind enough to give us different gifts. To be minimalist, we avoid unnecessary activities and things in our lives. You cannot use the word minimalist to mean that you are being rude to someone. Your responsibility as a minimalist is to explain the idea of minimalism and politely decline an offer. Tell them you don't need this product and it may not be useful in your home. You might suggest that the product be donated to a charity to help those in dire need. This donation could allow the recipient to make use of it. Encourage your family and friends, to give that product you don't want. If you are able to politely explain the situation to your family members and friends, they will likely understand and be willing and able to help you maintain a minimalist home.

Be always confident about your lifestyle.

It's not common to live a minimalist life. While minimalism isn't widely accepted and spread, it is now. However, many people have begun to realize the beauty of this lifestyle, and are now willing to accept its philosophy. This unique lifestyle will allow people to live differently, even in a constantly competitive world. We are used a lifestyle that involves buying large houses and expensive cars and presenting ourselves as cool. However, don't let this stop you from deciding if these items are needed. Minimalism helps us be strong in every aspect of our lives. Being minimalist allows us to be open to others who are not in agreement with our values, but it does not mean that we should change our lives. A minimalist should be confident that the lifestyle you choose will work for your happiness. Let's suppose your friend doesn't prefer a minimalist life style. Do you want to defend him/her? Just explain the meaning and why minimalism is important to you, and then mention how much you would like to live that way. You will be able to face others who are only trying to be rude if you keep this practice.

It is essential to have a positive outlook in order to live a minimalist and minimalist life. In order to free yourself from unnecessary clutter in your home and life, you must remove them all. Continue to review and update your possessions as well as the products in your house. You can find inspiration and guidance from minimalists. Keep reading blogs and books to find more ways to create a minimalist environment and lifestyle. A new friend or community member may be an inspiration to you and help you run your minimalist life with ease and mental peace. This will enable you to successfully maintain your minimalist house.

www.ingramcontent.com/pod-product-compliance
Lightning Source LLC
Chambersburg PA
CBHW050406120526
44590CB00015B/1850